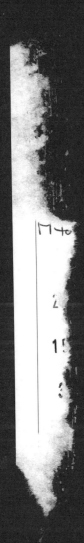

M40

2

15

3

WELSH JOURNEYS

First Impression
2005

ISBN 1 84323 569 2
© text: Jamie Owen
© photographs of the journey: Martin Cavaney
© other photographs: individual
photographs as noted, namely
Terry Beggs, Glyn Davies Photography,
Dyfed Elis-Gruffydd, Aled Hughes,
Steve Lewis, Jeremy Moore

(photo right: Aled Hughes)

Designed by MO-design.com

Printed in Wales at Gomer Press,
Llandysul, Ceredigion SA44 4JL
www.gomer.co.uk

WELSH JOURNEYS

JAMIE OWEN

PHOTOGRAPHS OF THE JOURNEY BY MARTIN CAVANEY

Gomer

CONTENTS

78

122

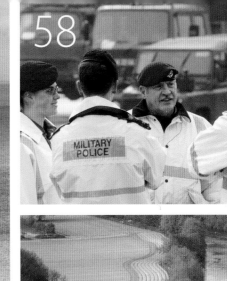

58

36

TŶ COCH INN

104

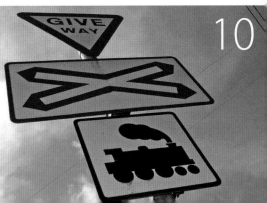

GIVE WAY

10

INTRODUCTION

When I said I would not be heading for Provence, Tuscany or the Greek Islands for my holidays but instead travelling through Wales, they laughed so much in the pub, they nearly died. Imagine the jokes – featuring hatchet-faced matronly ladies presiding over grim bed and breakfasts and monsoon-like, torrential rain.

It's indicative of an age of cheap flights that the very idea of exploring home is viewed as slightly barking. But ever since I wrote about my sailing voyages around the islands of Wales and later our coastal harbours, I've been struck again and again by how little we know about destinations closer to home. I guess it's often easier to join the airport queue. But I profoundly believe that in doing so you'll miss treasure under your nose. I've travelled all over the world but I don't mind telling you that standing on Snowdon's summit at sunset really does take a bit of beating.

This is the account of six journeys though Wales in the summer of 2005. Some areas like the Brecon Beacons were familiar to me; others, like the vale of Llangollen in Denbighshire, were new. Any discerning reader will wonder what travel journal from Wales would be complete without Pembrokeshire, the islands of Wales or the coast. They are indeed among the places I love most, and I had the opportunity to share my explorations of them in my last two books, so this time they are absent.

This isn't a guide book or a history of Wales but simply the story of my personal journeys, and the stories of the people I met along the way. Some of it is more autobiographical than I had thought it would be – I don't know what it is about writing about the landscape but it stirs in me a desire to remember and recall, as much as to record what I see. Above all, the book is a celebration of a beautiful country during one wonderful summer.

I was joined by a television crew making the series of this book. Christopher Howells, our director; cameramen Jon Rees, Richard Bartley, and Richard Longstaff; sound recordists Dafydd Parry and Richard Gott, assistant producer Emma Nunn and researcher Alex Howells. And, of course, by Martin Cavaney, the patient and longsuffering photographer of our journeys. They were all foolish enough to decline more glamorous assignments to share tents, youth hostels and holiday chalets on this adventure and despite everything were wonderful and amusing company.

I wrote copious notes between breaks in filming, at lunchtimes in pubs and before going to bed. My hope is that, put with the stunning photographic images assembled here, these jottings will convey the beauty and variety of Wales – both to those who know Wales well and to those who are yet to visit. I carried with me on these journeys many books written years ago by travellers to the same locations and it has been a pleasure to include some of their writing in this book.

I hope you enjoy reading it – oh, and by the way, do you know it rained only once.

Jamie Owen, 2005

THE HEART OF WAL

FROM A RAILWAY CARRIAGE

I love railway journeys, trains and stations – although the admission usually makes people move away, as though I were confessing to dressing up in women's clothes. Don't get me wrong, I'm not one of those kagool-wearers on the platform with tongue hanging out at the sight of a dirty old diesel. But I do enjoy the history and romance of railways.

Aled Hughes

Cynghordy viaduct

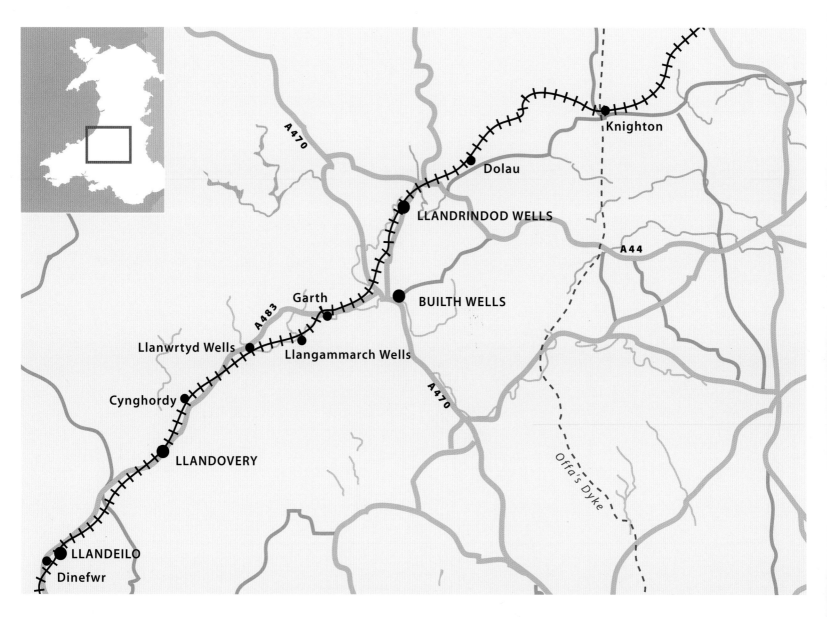

IT HAS BEEN A LONG LOVE AFFAIR, AND
it's in the blood. In the age of steam, my grandfather
was a driver on the Great Western Railway from
London to Pembroke Dock. Many years later, when my
father was left in charge of his three small boys (usually
when he had been particularly naughty himself), one of
our regular jaunts with him was to the station yard in
Pembroke Dock, where he would enthusiastically take
us to the ruins of the railway turntable. It was where the
steam locomotives would once have been spun around
and pointed back in the direction they'd just come from.

Those afternoons out with Dad were always visits to
wide-open spaces where we could make a lot of noise
without upsetting anyone (and we did make a lot of
noise), and they were also the places where he had spent
his own childhood, when the town had been a
prosperous busy place. Pembroke Dock station in
decline made him gloomy. 'Why don't people use the
trains any more?' he would complain as we all climbed
back into the Mini.

Well, I won't be needing my car keys for the next couple
of days. For about 120 miles from Swansea to
Shrewsbury the Heart of Wales Railway line trundles
through some of the most beautiful and unspoiled
landscape in Britain, and this is my chance to sit back
and gaze at it. The winding route passes three
mountains, two stunning viaducts and disappears into
seven tunnels. This is magnificent country for walking,
birdwatching, fishing, and just wandering. I have to tell
you, this is not a part of Wales I know well but I've
always thought of mid Wales as escape country – a long
way away from the seriousness of cities. This is wild

The Heart of Wales line

Llandeilo

country, alternative Britain, where the day's entertainment could offer bog snorkelling, a Morris Dancing festival, a chance to feed raw meat to birds of prey or dress up as one's great-great grandad during Victorian week. It wouldn't happen in London or Cardiff. I'm heading for the place where the eccentrics live.

The Heart of Wales line has been under threat of closure for years but as with all the best cliff-hangers, it always survives at the last moment. Wales lost miles of its railways under the pruning of Dr Beeching in the 1960s when it was thought that the rising numbers of car owners couldn't justify hundreds of miles of railways run at a loss. Beeching believed that Britain's railways should operate as a business not as a public service. The Heart of Wales line's great fortune was that it passed through marginal constituencies where axing the line would have been political hara-kiri. So it survived. And why does this little railway, which seems to owe more to Ivor the Engine than a modern business, still run today? How does it beguile all those hard-nosed accountants? The answer is that passenger numbers are growing, and the line is marketed as a tourist trip rather than a

transport service. So it's holding its own, just, and I want to travel on it not just for the sake of the journey but because there is something wonderfully romantic about the fact that the railway is here at all, against all odds.

The railway was primarily built to connect the industrial centres of the north-west of England with the then flourishing ports of south Wales. Industry was the primary motivator for the splendid feats of civil engineering through some of the most challenging mountains and valleys of Wales, but later it was tourism, and in particular the spa towns of Llandrindod, Llangammarch and Llanwrtyd, that would drum up passengers for the trains.

I'm starting my train travels in Llandeilo, and in the best traditions of well-planned railway journeys, I haven't got a timetable yet. I eventually find the railway station hidden, unloved, down a small lane, beyond once grand buildings now well past their prime. At the start of this momentous railway journey I feel as though there should be porters hurrying across platforms with trolleys piled high with beaten leather suitcases, or there might be couples staring longingly at each other in a crowded tearoom . . . but there are none of those things. In fact, there's no one here. Just me. A quick perusal of the timetable explains all – I've missed the train and there's not another for hours.

Time to kill and I know where I want to go. There's a beautiful country house, castle and park just minutes from here – Dinefwr Castle and Newton House set in stunning parkland. Dinefwr was the court of the medieval kingdom of Deheubarth, the southern kingdom of Wales, and the seat of the Welsh prince Lord Rhys, warrior, statesman and patron of the arts. Dinefwr Park is home to one of the greatest collections of ancient trees in Britain, some of them thought to be 700 years old. The deer park is only one of three remaining medieval enclosed deer parks in Wales.

The walk from the car park beside the great house to the castle is stunning; ancient trees heavy in leaf line the path, and grazing cattle watch disinterestedly before you start puffing uphill. From the battlements of the castle, I can see smoke rising slowly from a farmyard on the far bank of the river Tywi. In the far distance, high on the hill, Paxton's Tower stares back up the river valley.

I don't recommend walking around the castle ruins, the parkland and the great house in an hour. There's enough to keep you here for days: an iron age fort, two roman forts, a twelfth-century castle and a seventeenth-century mansion. But it's the buried history that I really want to see at Dinefwr. The newspapers this summer have been full of reports of the excavation here. Historians are ripping up their textbooks and the story of the Romans' time in Wales is having to be rewritten because of what they've discovered here. It had been thought that the Romans had an easy time controlling

Paxton's Tower

stuff – the Queen was Head of the Church and the country was on edge, fearful of the Catholic threat from continental Europe. Penry was arrested and executed aged 30 in 1593; he left a widow and four young daughters.

Although the church at Llangammarch dates from just before the First World War it contains some memorials from an earlier building and they speak of an extraordinary flowering of talent. In the eighteenth century, the living of Llangammarch was held by Theophilus Evans, the author of one of the first history books written in Welsh, Drych y Prif Oesoedd (Mirror of Ancient Times), first published in 1716.

Before he became vicar of Llangammarch, Theophilus Evans served as chaplain to the Gwynne family of Garth who later became stalwart supporters of Howel Harris and the Wesley brothers, the founders of Methodism. Marmaduke Gwynne came to Harris's rescue when he faced trumped-up charges (and a furious mob) at the Radnorshire quarter sessions in 1741; eight years later his daughter Sarah married Charles Wesley, the great hymn writer and brother of John, who performed the marriage service. The tiny church of Llanlleonfel, on the hillside above the A483(T) a short distance west of Garth House, has memorials to members of the Gwynne family and a modern tablet recording the marriage of Sarah and Charles.

Between Llanwrtyd and Builth Wells the railway passes close to a cluster of places of great significance in the cultural and religious history of Wales, most of which are relatively unknown today.

John Penry was a defiant critic of the Elizabethan church which he saw as corrupt and misgoverned. His birthplace, Cefn-brith, can still be seen two miles east of Llanwrtyd. He wrote bitter, provocative pamphlets in the 1580s and '90s against bishops and the failure of the clergy to minister to their people; this was dangerous

Statue of John Penry
Llangammarch churchyard

west Wales but the excavation of this fort suggests that the locals perhaps gave the conquerers more grief than previously imagined. On the far side of the park, a dozen heads bob above the grass. The dig is in full swing.

Dr Emma Plunkett Dillon, the National Trust's archaeologist, is knee-deep in a trench. The Romans were predictable builders, she explains. They built forts at the end of a day's march, so if you know where two forts are, you can discover where the missing one might be. Historians have known there must be a Roman fort somewhere in Llandeilo but were not sure where until now. The archaeologists have discovered a fort that included several banks and ditches and perhaps a bath-house. Their geophysical survey also suggests that the fort was superimposed over an earlier larger fort with a slightly different alignment. It's the most extraordinary feeling standing here knowing that a Roman soldier could have stood in the same place two thousand years ago and wondered, 'Is the tea shop open?'

Back at Llandeilo station the 'up' platform for stations to Shrewsbury is on the far side of the station which means a walk over the twin tracks, as there is no pedestrian bridge here. I still get a *frisson* when walking across a railway track. The other waiting passengers, about a dozen in number, are mostly retired and quite unconcerned that the service from Swansea will be twelve minutes late. This is an adventure where time and punctuality matter little. We know where we are going, and it doesn't matter terribly when we arrive.

A two-tone siren in the distance has all of us on alert and then the train's yellow front comes into view. When

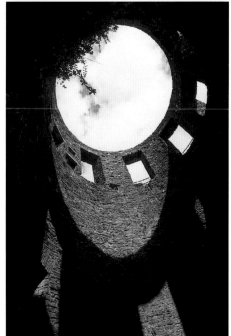

Newton House and Dinefwr Castle; Roman dig; return to the Heart of Wales train

Above: The Black Mountain, below: Myddfai

it arrives at the platform it looks more like a bus than a train, and there's only one carriage. I'm not sure what I expected for my railway journey but I try not to look disappointed as two white-shirted staff jump out and enjoy a moment's fresh air before the metal tube continues on its way.

There are already dozens of passengers on-board from Swansea. But we all find a perch soon and so begins the ritual of laying out food and books, newspapers and drinks. The train doesn't leave with much ceremony; just a quiet digital beep and we're on our way with a jolt.

From Llandeilo the railway follows the Tywi valley past Rhosmaen, Cwmifor, Bethlehem and Felindre. Carreg Cennen Castle is resplendent at the foot of the Black Mountain, which we will skirt along for miles. It's difficult to imagine a more dramatic setting for the beginning of a journey.

An elderly couple sit opposite with a steaming flask and a huge picnic, enough for an adventure across Europe: brown bread sandwiches, shiny pork pies and a sponge cake. She's wearing a pink beret pinned jauntily to one side of her head. He's in a straw hat. They hardly speak a word for ages but seem deliriously happy in each other's company. They must have been married for years and they know what the other is thinking. I hope they can't read my mind, because I'm starving and gagging for a slice of that sponge.

A French girl, no doubt a student, sits opposite me, immersed in maps and guidebooks. She's 'doing Britain'. She's tanned and very beautiful and I hope she can't read my mind either otherwise she'll be banging her fists on the doors trying to escape.

Two rows away a spread of *The Guardian* occasionally reveals a bearded man, his gaze drifting off to the green hills. A couple of sisters on holiday from London talk non-stop, oblivious to any scenery.

There's no buffet car but the passengers are well prepared, their tables laden with flasks and bottles, sandwiches wrapped in silver foil and old sweet tins full of small cakes. Mr and Mrs Hulme from Swansea are on a day out to Shrewsbury. Mr Hulme worked on the railways all his life and his punishment in retirement is a goodbye gift of subsidised rail travel.

The French girl (whose name I've discovered is Nici) becomes unsettled at every station, unsure of where to change trains. My efforts in awful French to assure her that I will personally carry her to her destination if she gets lost obviously lose something in translation, and she looks even more unsettled than before.

Those who've enjoyed a good lunch are getting comfortable for a snooze. Both the sisters and the old couple are fast asleep, mouths open, when the conductor checks our tickets. He leaves the sleepers to their slumbers. He tries to explain to Nici where she has to change trains, sharing the intricacies of Britain's railway timetables. It's like watching an earthling and a martian debate physics.

The Guardian reader is, I think, a novelist, writing copiously in a beautiful leather-bound work book. His industry makes my few notes after so many hours look paltry. The fact is, I'm good at being idle. The windows are a feast for the eyes, the Welsh countryside at its brushed-up best. In the fields around Manordeilo, the grass is being turned in the sun. It's forecast to be one

Above: Tywi valley, below: Black Mountain slopes

Llywelyn Ap Gruffydd
Fychan

They [the Welsh people] value themselves much on their antiquity, the ancient race of their houses, families and the like, and above all, their ancient heroes . . . and, as they believe their country to be the pleasantest and most agreeable in the world, so you cannot oblige them more than to make them think that you believe so too.

Daniel Defoe, *Tour through the Whole Island of Great Britain*, 1724

Martin Caxaney

Monument to Llywelyn ap Gruffydd at Llandovery

Llandovery

carry large sums of money from market to landowners. And so modern banking was born here in Llandovery. Fancy that.

Llandovery was also a large coaching town, an important centre on the turnpike road to London (now the A40) between the 1780s and 1850s. This is where the horses would be changed and travellers kicked off their boots and enjoyed the 47 pubs that were recorded here in 1822. I down a good dinner where the drovers and coach-travellers once sat and drank, then it's an early night for me, so if you'll excuse me, I'm putting out the light. Nos Da.

of the hottest days of the summer so far. We pass Llangadog and Llanwrda, then the gentle sprint and fast tickety-tick of the train slows to an unenthusiastic jog: we're arriving in Llandovery.

After the air-conditioned railway carriage, the heat of the afternoon is a welcome delight. The Heart of Wales railway track shimmers in waving lines in the straight mile out of the station. The dirty yellow backside of the train waddles away in hazy fumes.

The King's Head Inn, which dates from the sixteenth century, nestles in the middle of town. It was once the home of Banc yr Eidion Du, the Black Ox Bank, a drovers' bank and the first in Wales. From the sixteenth century, the head drover had to be licensed and only men over the age of 30, married, and householders could apply. The head drover had to be entirely trust-worthy, as he carried large sums of cash after cattle sales. It was a risky undertaking. One enterprising drover, David Jones, dreamed up the idea of a drovers' bank so it would no longer be necessary to

At seven o'clock in the morning, a steady procession of Landrovers and cattle lorries arrives at Llandovery mart. Some farmers tow small horseboxes, others arrive in large trucks, all of them carrying sheep to market. The auctioneer Derfel Harries says prices are not good for lambs this week because the weather's too hot and no one wants to cook meat in this heat. The sellers jump out of their vehicles clutching triplicate sheets of paper that accompany all livestock movements. Signing and checking done, the trailer doors are opened to reveal confused and loud lambs which pause before rushing towards the weighing pens. Some lambs are scrubbed to look like an advertisement for knitting wool, others are encaked in the muck of living on the hills. All of the dozen or so farmers, their wives and mart staff know each other. This is a regular and familiar day for them, starting with 'Bore da' and a hand-shake, some tittle-tattle, and possibly exchange useful intelligence on another mart's prices up the road. But there is a sense of old-fashioned good manners here

– dignity, formality and etiquette dominate the proceedings. The auctioneer and his staff and many of the farmers wear tweed jackets and ties.

The farmers grumble about getting the same price for a lamb as they did ten years ago, but I've never seen such happy, healthy people. It may be a hard life but this lot won't be exchanging it for another. Two of the farmers leaning against the pen reminisce about driving cattle on foot here through the streets of Llandovery, bringing the town to a standstill. The majority of the men and women watching the sale begin are over fifty – and you do get a sense of the end of an era. At the coffee stall, a farmer from Carmarthenshire complains that all the acreage around him near Bethlehem is being sold to incomers who want the country life but not the responsibility of farming.

The auction begins. I had expected a theatre of waving and shouting but this is a subtler game of almost imperceptible movements of face and hands. The sale of hundreds of Welsh lambs takes place with good nature, a few jokes and gentle ribbing. It's the parting of company of farmer and his animals after months of care – feeding, watering and watching. The dispatching is over in the space of an hour, in a scene that you could have watched at any time in the last five hundred years.

The lambs are sold for about £50 each, mostly to the local abattoir which has a contract with a supermarket. Some of the animals will be sold as halal meat which is a growing market for Welsh farmers. The lambs which trotted in here an hour ago will be on shop shelves tomorrow and on dinner plates the following day. Which reminds me – it must be time for breakfast.

The mart at Llandovery

Cynghordy viaduct

The cobbled square outside the King's Head looks on to the arched town hall and fountain, and it's a shame that on this hottest of summers no one has put some tables out in the sun to offer food and drink. In France or Italy a space like this would be humming with customers in need of a sit down and some refreshment. In Wales we seem to have a peculiarly nonconformist fear of being seen enjoying ourselves outdoors.

Time to catch the Heart of Wales line again, the second service of the day.

Our route takes us along the Brân valley, west of Pentre-tŷ-gwyn and Babel and the side of Crychan Forest, before we witness one of the most spectacular sights of this railway journey: the viaduct at Cynghordy, on the southern edge of the Cambrian Mountains.

As we pull into Llanwrtyd Wells the gaggle of waiting passengers make the flowered platform look untidy. The station's hanging baskets and borders are glorious. There's a Morris Dancing festival on here today, which we haven't particularly come to see but as it's lunchtime and we're all in need of a bite to eat, it could be fun. Llanwrtyd Wells claims to be the smallest town in Britain, with only six hundred residents according to the last census. Like so many of the towns on the Heart of Wales line, it owes its existence to the mineral waters and to the tourists who once came here to cure themselves of anaemia, malaria and gout. Each of the spa towns offered slightly different cures and the crowds flocked in.

Theophilus Evans, a local clergyman, is credited with discovering the mineral waters here at Llanwrtyd –

Above: Foxgloves through the window, below: Llanwrtyd Wells station

THE DROVERS

All over Wales there are pubs called 'The Drovers' or 'The Drovers Arms'. They mark stages on the many routes along which cows, sheep and other livestock, including geese, were taken from west Wales to the fattening pastures and markets of the English Midlands and London.

The animals were herded along broad tracks which converge on droving centres like Tregaron, Llandovery and Beulah before setting off for England. The trade was enormously influential in pre-industrial Wales; John Williams, archbishop of York during the Civil Wars, compared the drovers to 'the Spanish fleet of North Wales which brings that little gold and silver we have', an allusion to the fabled wealth of the treasure fleet from the New World which fuelled Spain's empire. A hundred years later the dangers of carrying large amounts of silver and gold from the sale of cattle and sheep back to Wales prompted the founding of banks which issued their own distinctive notes; Banc-y-Ddafad-Ddu at Aberystwyth had, as its name suggests, sheep or lambs on its currency. In the days before the railways spread newspapers nationwide the drovers were important sources of news, and no doubt a good deal of gossip and scandal about the wicked world beyond Wales.

The drovers' way of life was made more difficult first by the introduction of the turnpike roads which charged a toll on all traffic including animals, then the rapid expansion of the railways which offered a much quicker form of transport. In November 1923 David Jones helped drive 750 lambs from Garth to Brecon; he got very wet and cold and recalled how pleased he was to reach the Drovers' Arms on the Epynt where the landlady had a good fire in front of which he dried out. This is a salutary reminder of the realities of the drovers' lives and warns us against romanticizing the past.

Above: Sculpture of a drover at Llandovery
Left: Drovers' road at Abergwesyn, Llandovery

Jeremy Moore

the product of foul-smelling springs. Legend has it that he watched a frog thrive in the sulphurous waters and so sampled it himself in the hope it would cure his scurvy. Don't try this at home.

Today the spa tourists may have gone but there are a handful of good reasons to still make Llanwrtyd your destination. Faced with competition from the cheaper, hotter costas and cut-price airlines the local landlords have come up with a diary of bizarre and headline-grabbing events to pull in the punters. The Man versus Horse contest was started by the landlord of the Neuadd Arms after overhearing a heated argument about who would win a race between a man and a horse. The world bog-snorkelling championships take place here, as does the real ale ramble and Morris in the forest, an annual get-together of Morris dancers from all over Britain.

As we walk along the main street of Llanwrtyd dozens of Morris dancers have brought the traffic to a standstill and a crowd of a hundred or so tourists look on somewhat bemused. A couple of dogs race alongside the dancers who have blackened their faces (tradition has it that, thus disguised, poor farm workers would beg for money). We make a dismal attempt to film an interview with a couple of the Morris dancers while they are dancing but Richard, the soundman, shakes his head, complaining about the havoc their crashing sticks and jingling bells are causing. It's a curious life that a man's livelihood should derive from a snatched exchange with a busy Morris dancer wearing tights and bells, trying to kick a dog that's taken exception to his kind of music, but it falls to me to have a go. Later, over a drink in the Neuadd Arms, the Morris dancers turn

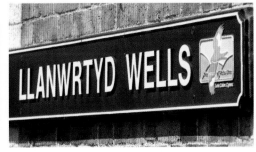

out to be a bunch of teachers, civil servants, bankers and office workers. I guess the weekends are reserved for breaking out and doing something wacky . . .

Llanwrtyd Wells

Filming done, it's time to belt back to the train. We make it just as it squeals into the station. It has to be said the Heart of Wales railway runs like clockwork – photographer Martin Cavaney says that's because it *is* clockwork. None of us would be surprised to see a large key in the side of the dinky carriage. No sooner do we settle back into our seats, speed up and then slow down, than it's time for another stop. We're not getting out here, but lots of old men with a speed that belies their years leap out of the train at Llangammarch Wells and

Aled Hughes

Memorial to Llywelyn ap Gruffydd at Cilmeri

begin photographing the train from the outside. I'm mystified but at the same time delighted by their passion. When we were little, my brothers and I had a Hornby train set in the attic where we would spend hours watching the trains go round. This must be the same addiction.

At Garth station a cyclist gets out of the carriage, his bike bending under the load of rucksack, tent and bedding. We stop for just seconds then doors close and we move onwards to Cilmeri where Llywelyn, last indigenous Prince of Wales, was betrayed and killed in 1282.

At Llandrindod Wells station the train driver hops out of his cab to exchange a token – the pass that gives our train the right of way up the single-track line. The convention hails from the early days of the railways and the myriad of accidents on single-track lines when apparently a policeman would hand his truncheon to the locomotive driver, authorising him alone safe passage along the line. Our driver today says all of his colleagues love working on this route. It's slow, stop-start stuff, but there's no stress and the scenery is stunning.

The bowling club at Llandrindod Wells has invited us for tea so it would be rude not to go. We leave the train and make our way to the manicured velvet lawns where sixty white-haired, white-clad bowlers battle it out with a competitiveness their age should have left behind. I've never watched bowls before but it's wonderfully soporific. The grass is freshly cut, there's a gentle clatter of applause, but even for victory the cheer is no louder than pianissimo.

This morning's newspapers were full of another tedious footballer's drugs and violence scandal. I wonder when we lost touch with sportsmanship and good manners in competition. The bowlers of Llandrindod are thrashing Lincolnshire – their opposition – but, so far, no one has sworn or huddled in a mass kiss on the green lawns.

When spa resorts were at their height well over a century ago, the well-to-do who travelled from all over Britain by train to Llandrindod came here to take the waters (which just goes to show that our modern obsession with health farms and healthy living is nothing new) but were also intent on having a good time. Llandrindod was marketed in its heyday as 'The Montpellier of Radnorshire'. Tourists here would have enjoyed all the trappings of their lives in town: dancing at balls, billiards, horse-racing – and, of course, bowls. Completion of the railway line in 1865 had provided ready access so that, twenty years later, a fairly inaccessible and remote little town had been transformed into a fashionable inland resort known as the 'Queen of the Welsh watering places'.

A brisk walk in the burning afternoon sun takes us back to the station. As the carriage pulls in, our faces look ludicrously red – we're all burnt after hours filming outside in the heat of the day. Back on-board, we settle among new passengers and unfamiliar train staff.

The Heart of Wales line has encouraged each town or village to adopt their local station, and the result is that every one is given tender loving care. Dolau station has been awarded the title of 'Best-kept station in Wales', which is some accolade on this line because every station we've visited has been spotless. Our

Llandrindod Wells, water sculpture

Dolau station

director Chris warns the film crew not to stand around on the platform here looking scruffy lest we are tidied up, and it's good advice.

The station's volunteers greet us at Dolau with all the enthusiasm of born-again evangelists. This is no ordinary station and the people who live here are extraordinary types. Some volunteers are hoeing the borders, others painting the fence, and nestled below the station sign, I spot a trestle-table heaving under a feast of *bara brith* and shortbread. There's even iced tea. There will be no more trains for hours now so we won't be troubled by noise and smells. It's so British and, of course, completely mad. The flower borders wouldn't disgrace Chelsea flower show, the lawns are beautifully trimmed and two flagpoles display the union flag and the Welsh dragon. If a meteor ever strikes Britain, Morris Minors, caravans and Dolau station will still be here after the clouds have parted.

We're not the only passengers disembarking; a group of ramblers huddle around a map, unsure of their bearings. I hope they move soon before someone gets the duster out. One of the train guards said to me earlier that Britain's railways would be great if they didn't have to cope with the needs of their passengers.

I suppose this is at the heart of our railways' conundrum in Britain: we love the railways as long as other people use them. We love the romance of a lost age of travel, its heritage, the Great Western Railway, the age of steam and cathedral-like Victorian stations. We love the idea of keeping cars off the road and keeping our cities free of traffic, but our love affair is with the idea of the railways, our passion is for an abstraction. By and large we don't use railways as daily transport, and when we do, we don't like the carriages full of other people with their noise and curious personal habits. But mention closing the railways and cutting lines or services and we become furious and proprietorial about them. They are a good thing, we think, even if we don't use them. And even if we don't use them now, we might use them – one day.

They'd never dare close the Heart of Wales line for fear of the fanatics like those at Dolau station turning up at headquarters and storming the building. Which brings me back to tea on the platform. Elspeth is cutting an enormous slice of home-made cake and pouring Earl Grey, best china cup and saucer in hand. Then it's time for a tour of the station, which I'm not expecting to take long. At the end of the platform a shelter resembling a garden shed is full of certificates from winning every best-kept station competition for years. Black and white photographs show the station in its heyday; there was once another platform, a goods yard, a general waiting room, a ladies waiting-room, and a lamp room, all gone now. (I read in the papers that the railways are considering reviving the Ladies waiting-rooms to make female passengers feel safer.) Robert Louis Stevenson's poem, 'From a Railway Carriage', hangs framed on the panelled wall. There's a visitors' book too, which is a first for me, I must admit. When was the last time you signed a visitors' book at a railway station? There are no old beer cans, no signs of vandalism and no graffiti.

My short tour over, it's time for a sandwich – and very nice they are too. Elspeth, a magnetic character who lives over the fence, says the Queen once came here by train on the way to the Royal Welsh Show. Her train stopped at the station but some flunky forgot to

Jeremy Moore

open the carriage blinds. Imagine the line-up of the great and the good on the platform, in their best dresses, all staring at a train with its blinds drawn.

Dolau is a piece of Britain that people think no longer exists, where a community ready to weed, prune and paint can work together to make a place that you'd think belongs to the past. But it belongs to the here and now, because that's what they want here, and that's what they've created. I feel privileged to have been a part of it, albeit for a short time.

After handshakes and thanks I wander over to the village's chapel across the road. Across the fence, a farmer arrives in his pick-up to herd sheep in the adjoining field.

The railway line borders the graveyard but the residents of Dolau Baptist Chapel cemetery are only disturbed four times a day. The grass has been freshly cut and the stalks around the gravestones trimmed. This plot is full of people who died young. John Williams died in 1878 aged 17; Richard Thomas aged one year, 5 months died in 1879; Sarah Stephen, 12 years, 1882; Elizabeth Hamer, 21 years, 1887. Such short lives. Dolau's generation lying here lived in a time before long life and good health were taken for granted.

The railway tracks are whistling, which I can tell you is an unnerving sound in a graveyard. The train's coming and it's time to say goodbye to Dolau.

The line takes us to Llanbister Road station, south of Pool Hill and past Llangunllo station. Knucklas viaduct is another breathtaking piece of engineering: thirteen arches and castellated turrets at each end. After only a few minutes and not many more miles, to my final destination, Knighton on Offa's Dyke.

Above left: Dolau Baptist Chapel cemetery, above right: Knucklas viaduct, below: Knighton

Knighton railway station was built for grander trains than ours. Its long platform looks faintly disgusted as the single carriage plods to its centre. I suddenly feel sorry to be getting off here. I've become entranced by the slow, mesmeric journey across so many hundreds of beautiful acres. I'd happily sit here and be hypnotised by more of the swaying and clicking of the train tomorrow. When I was a little boy I spent years wishing the years away so I could learn to drive and enjoy the freedom that it brought. Now I adore slouching in front of this glorious canvas of countryside, staring out through the window and letting someone else decide on my journey.

Knighton railway station is in England but the town itself lies in Wales. The Visitors' Centre in Knighton is devoted to the history of Offa's Dyke itself, this great monument that runs down the whole length of Wales. For the sake of the camera we stand on the road bridge over the railway tracks and play a game of hokey-kokey, walking back and forth across the border with England. It's the quickest and easiest border crossing we could ever make. Then a siren blasts below us and we peer over the bridge to watch the train departing from Knighton station – and leaving Wales.

There is something splendidly British about a railway that doesn't go anywhere much, has few passengers, is slow and costs a fortune in subsidies. But you have to look beyond all that to realise that Wales would be poorer without the Heart of Wales line. I don't suppose mine would count as one of the great railway journeys of the world but as small railway journeys go, this has been a great one. And now I'll stop, before you think I've turned into a train-spotter.

Knighton; Heart of Wales line

FROM A RAILWAY CARRIAGE

Faster than fairies, faster than witches,
Bridges and houses, hedges and ditches;
And charging along like troops in a battle
All through the meadows the horses and cattle:
All of the sights of the hill and the plain
Fly as thick as driving rain;
And ever again, in the wink of an eye,
Painted stations whistle by.

Here is a child who clambers and scrambles,
All by himself and gathering brambles;
Here is a tramp who stands and gazes;
And there is the green for stringing the daisies!
Here is a cart run away in the road
Lumping along with man and load;
And here is a mill, and there is a river:
Each a glimpse and gone for ever!

Robert Louis Stevenson (1850-94)

Aled Hughes

From Cynghordy viaduct

THE WYE VALLEY

Jeremy Moore

KAYAKING DOWNRIVER

Standing by the river an hour before my kayaking adventure begins, I'm relieved to see that the Wye looks still as a millpond. I can't gauge its speed or direction but at least the river looks docile. In the same way that a boxer watches his opponent moments before the bell, I feel a sense of quiet and mounting confidence.

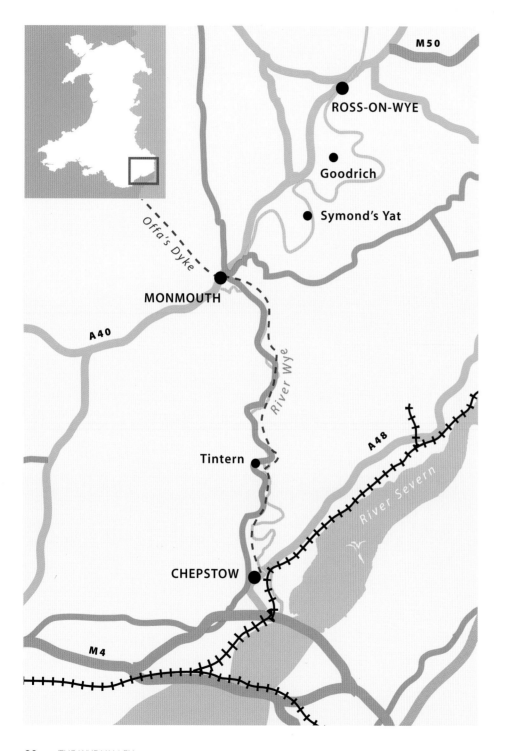

ROSS-ON-WYE

Goodrich

Symond's Yat

Offa's Dyke

MONMOUTH

A40

River Wye

Tintern

A48

River Severn

CHEPSTOW

M4

M50

JESS CAN HARDLY BE MUCH MORE THAN seventeen, and only a seal could be more adept on the water. She has the heavy task of giving me a crash course in kayaking so that I can safely paddle down the Wye for two days without drowning. In the same way that children help their wobbly grandparents down steps, she guides me through a few unsteady hours afloat. It's years since I sat in a kayak so I feel rather timid being shovelled into a plastic aperture not much wider than a jar. My requests for a porky-broadcaster-size vessel meet with a look of mounting concern.

There is a diversity of hoped-for outcomes from a documentary like the one we're filming. The director Chris Howells, cameraman Richard Bartley and stills photographer Martin Caveney all hope for disaster of Titanic proportions – it will make 'good pictures'. I, on the other hand, on no account want to deliver hilarious out-takes for decades to come. In that spirit of divided ambitions, our filming begins.

Once I'm on the water, the gentle flow observed from the bank transforms into current fast enough to give a passing bicycle a run for its money. Simply trying to balance in the seat makes my back ache. I'm not a natural, and the physical effort of trying to maintain correct posture, the right stroke and not falling in is made all the more difficult by the crew wanting shots from the other side of the river. It's as much as I can do to stay upright, let alone go in a direction of my choosing. And then there are the swans – go anywhere near them when they're on the nest and you take your life in your hands. Every swan in the world seems to have set up shop on the river Wye this summer – must be swan 'extras' hired by the director to give a bit of edge.

As you ask, the lesson is progressing well: I can turn, back-paddle and shift in my seat without capsizing. Then I mis-paddle – and scoop what seems like a gallon of water into the kayak. I try not to look as though I've got a soaking wet backside while a swan begins an intelligence-gathering mission in my direction.

My lesson on the river passes off without failure or distinction. My instructor Jess leaps back into the water to resume her former life as a fish, and I wander around Ross-on-Wye with water dripping from my shorts.

This really is a beautiful little town. When you drive over the ancient Wilton stone bridge, Ross-on-Wye looks lofty and aloof, standing proud on red cliffs as though waiting for an ocean to wash its dusty face. St Mary's Church steeple dominates the blue sky for miles around. The church is open, which is rare these days, but Ross feels like the kind of place that couldn't possibly harbour church burglars. It's the stained glass that is St Mary's treasure: one window portrays Joseph holding the infant Christ, a scene not unique but unusual. The glass in the east window dates from 1430.

The old market house stands on stout, sandstone pillars looking down on a twisting main street. At the time of the Domesday Book, this was a small village below the wooded hills of Chase and Penyard, a manor of the Bishops of Hereford. By the eighteenth century, Ross had developed as a popular destination for travellers seeking the picturesque scenery of the river Wye. Lord Nelson was among the visitors here.

There's a wonderful old bookshop in Ross, not the usual chain store affair with bright lights and top ten best sellers, but one of those delightful places straight

Above: Jess, kayak instructor; first lesson; below: Ross-on-Wye

The bookshop and its treasures, Ross-on-Wye

out of Dickens. Small window panes, the reek of old leather and damp pages. Sarah Threader owns Ross Old Book and Print Shop and the ancient shelves conceal a business which is carried out on the Internet, trading throughout the world. I tell Sarah about our journey and she burrows around for a guidebook to the river Wye written in 1892. We agree it would be fun to follow a journey by river that someone else wrote a century ago. Her parting gift is the news that the son of one of the authors is in the area and would be fascinated to hear of our journey. She makes a phone call and all is arranged.

Michael Goffe, son of one of the medical students who wrote *Camping on the Wye*, tells the story of how, in 1892, a group of four undergraduates from University College, London set off on a boating and camping trip, hiring a skiff in Hereford and taking it by goods train to Whitney with all their stores. Their journey was recorded in a sketchbook and diary – a glorious celebration of various camp-sites by the river, battles with bugs, insects and nosey cows, and all the highs and lows of a river journey.

In a beer garden by the river, Michael reads from the opening of the journal, his mellow voice painting the pictures for us, as though we had walked back in time

'A bell tent was secured . . . two rugs, waterproof sheets, tinned plates, mugs etc, and kit bags for each man, and a spirit cooking stove for three persons secured. Groceries with the inevitable tinned meat were ordered to be ready at Paddington. All the able bodied men in the village came round to assist in conveying us to the river and an imposing procession took place: G in college blazer and B with Banjo,

Wilton Bridge

H distributed ample largesse and the boat gradually sank with our packing until it rested on the bottom and much heaving was necessary to get her off.'

I can't stop laughing at the splendid images or perhaps it's hysteria at the prospect of my own likely bungling. Michael is wonderful company and I agree to keep the book in my kayak as a constant companion over the next few days.

It is morning on Wye Street outside the Hope and Anchor pub where it is too early for the regulars to even contemplate the first drink of the day. We gather to begin our kayaking trip down the Wye which today looks glossy and green, reflecting the wall of overhanging trees on its banks. The flag of St George hangs limply on a flag-pole above empty beer casks. This is England, but only just. This will be the slowest border crossing I have ever made but, by the end of our journey in Chepstow, we will have arrived in Wales.

There are two television crews. One will follow my journey from the land, filming wide shots for the programme, and the other will be in another kayak a few hundred yards behind me. Richard, our soundman, puts a small microphone and battery on my shirt just so he can record the sound of paddling and my panting exhaustion. I'm hoping that in the event of capsizing I won't get electrocuted. 'Just as long as I've got clean sound it won't matter if you are,' he says. In a move that silences the small crowd on the bank, Richard gets out a pack of condoms and starts unrolling one. 'This is to cover the expensive microphone on the life-jacket to save it getting wet,' he explains. The good people of Ross move away from us very quickly.

Life-jacket strapped firmly on and stores on board, I push off in front of the remaining well-wishers. I must admit I do feel a gathering sense of privilege to be involved in this caper.

I know Ross is well behind me now, but I daren't look back because I'll overturn. In front of me are the ancient red arches of Wilton bridge – the main road from Fishguard to London. In the eighteenth and nineteenth centuries, this river-bank would have been home to rope-makers, basket-weavers and boat-builders. It would have reeked of horses towing barges up and down the river carrying goods to Hereford, Monmouth and Chepstow. Pleasure boats left from here to carry visitors to admire the Wye gorge.

After relaxing into my strokes I'm gripped with a sudden shudder of apprehension at the thought of navigating my passage under a bridge. I can see that some arches have fast water running through them, others show stones close to the surface. My honeymoon period is about to come to an abrupt end. In a totally incompetent sweep with my paddle I manage to scoop a

Kerne Bridge

bucketful of river into my kayak which leaves cold water sloshing around my backside once again. My map and Michael's book are soaked.

The bridge passes without incident, however. A small victory, but it marks progress in my kayaking career.

I feel a rising sense of relaxation after another hour. Thankfully, the flow of the water is strong enough to propel me along without doing much more than a few corrective strokes. Burning sunshine and the gentle slosh of water passing by lulls you very quickly into a relaxed state. All is well with the world this morning.

The medical students back in 1892 camped in Goodrich Castle. These days it's run by English Heritage and I suspect they'd set the dogs on me if I unrolled my sleeping bag there. On the river-bank opposite the castle, a dozen or so easels are lined up and a tall, distinguished man dressed in white moves between seated painters. I have to confess a deep admiration of anyone who can paint. Some members of the art class are painting the scene as I see it – a broad prospect of

river, castle and hills. Others catch a fragment of water or field and ignore the wide vista. Brushes, canvas and a jar of water is all that these painters need. The place is as beautiful now as when Turner came here to paint in 1792.

The first castle at Goodrich was recorded in the Norman Domesday Survey. It had a great strategic importance because it overlooked and controlled an important ford across the Wye. It's strange how the passage of time changes perception of the landscape. When this place was built it was constructed to put the fear of God into the locals. Now this ruin of red sandstone gladdens the heart and lifts the spirit. In the fields, acres of plastic poly-tunnels shelter fruit from the worst a British summer might have in store. This week, it's hot enough for the strawberries to cook on the chocolate earth.

After the grand high arches of Kerne Bridge the river runs almost straight past Thomas Wood. After an hour, the Wye almost turns back on itself to make a peninsula called Welsh Bicknor. (Another village nearby called English Bicknor is a clue to our proximity to a once fought-over borderland.) The church at Welsh Bicknor no longer has a congregation and the cemetery belongs to the nettles and long grass. No one tends its wobbly wooden porch or its fallen fence, yet for all its decay, it's a place of beauty and tranquility. No wonder they built a church here: it's close to heaven.

We're a world away from roads and the only sound now is frantic birdsong. Pink campions line the bank as though someone were dressing the place for dinner. The blossom is coming on the trees, white and red on green. The breeze blows the smell of wild garlic and mown grass. We are to sleep here tonight in a tepee on the river-bank. I can't imagine anywhere more perfect. When the campers of 1892 stayed near here, they saw a sight that none of us hope to see: 'In the village a travelling bear was amusing the youngsters.' The students had already come under the spell of the river Wye and enjoyed wandering!

'In the afternoon we explored the fields and met a young farmer harvesting who led us though apple orchards alive with geese and turkeys. He was very hospitable and we sat in his garden and drank cyder and talked through the afternoon. His family (butterfly catching) came round to the tent which the ladies had already inspected during our absence and remarked that they thought a woman might have made the place look more comfortable.'

I fall asleep before reading much more, exhausted by today's exercise.

It's breakfast time and director Howells points in the direction of the Youth Hostel nearby. The hostel is the

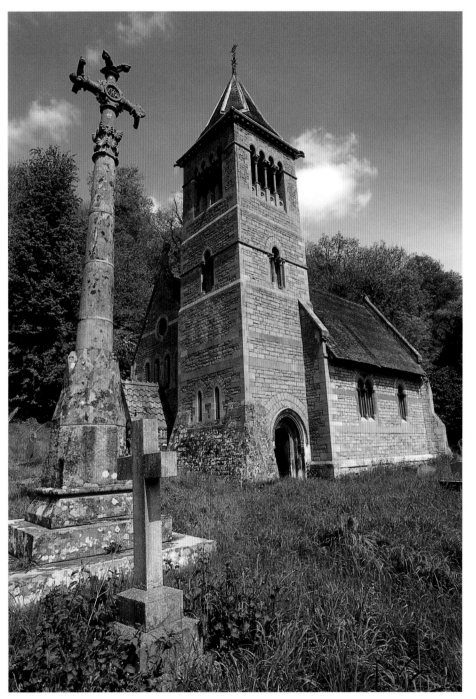

Welsh Bicknor

INDUSTRY IN THE WYE VALLEY

Visitors to Ironbridge on the Severn in Shropshire are immediately struck by the wooded beauty and tranquillity of the site and it takes some time to appreciate that this was once a cradle of industry. The same is true – but to a lesser degree – of the Wye near Tintern. Most of our impressions of industry are based on the nineteenth century, with towering mills and chimneys belching smoke, surrounded by densely-populated towns; this is not what industry was like in the sixteenth to eighteenth centuries. Then the most potent source of power was provided by rivers and streams, the fuel was charcoal as often as coal, and the workforce was small.

Two streams which join the Wye – the White Brook and the Angidy above Llandogo and at Tintern, respectively – supplied the power for a variety of small industrial enterprises. Archaeologists and historians have identified a series of revealing sites in these two narrow valleys. They include the wireworks which operated from the sixteenth century, a blast furnace, waterwheels and mill pools, warehouses and wharves. In the eighteenth century paper-making took over on the White Brook as the main employment, whereas ironworking lasted longer at Tintern (there is still a Furnace farm on the Angidy a mile west of Tintern). However, these small-scale works were faced with fierce competitors when the greater resources of the Heads of the Valleys began to be exploited and Merthyr Tydfil, Dowlais, Tredegar and Ebbw Vale were established as the new centres of industrial power.

Until the coming of the railways, the Wye, like all the navigable rivers of Britain, was a vital transport artery linking inland towns to the ports. Sir Richard Colt Hoare, an inveterate traveller, came to Llandogo in 1797 and commented that, 'Spring tides come up here and vessels of 100 ton burthen'. He made little further comment on the industrial activities close to the Wye as he was more interested in the Picturesque attractions of the scenery which had so captivated Wordsworth and Turner.

former vicarage, built at a time when the bishops believed in God and the clergy lived like kings. The congregation at breakfast this morning are mostly the active elderly clad in lycra cycling shorts, our televison crew, and a couple of brooding serial killers on holiday. We scoff an enormous amount of bacon, sausages, eggs and toast. It's hungry work, this kayaking.

My destination this morning is Symonds Yat. Here the river banks have become steep, like cliffs of a gorge. Symonds Yat Rock is over five hundred feet above sea level and the view is panoramic. On this clear blue day, I can see Coety Mountain near Blaenafon some twenty miles away and the Black Mountains at a similar distance. From here the Wye below me looks like a narrow stream, still and shadowed.

Around me birdwatchers with binoculars watch peregrine falcons scan the acres below us for wood pigeon and starling, unaware of their impending death in the beak of the fastest creature on Earth. That the peregrines are here at all is a tribute to the RSPB; they were gone thirty years ago, killed off by pesticides, but they've now returned to their old haunts.

Standing here, looking at the Wye hundreds of feet below, I suddenly can't help thinking about where the water has been and where it's going. I'm kayaking the fifth longest river in Britain; the water passing below me gathered on the slopes of Pumlumon at the Wye's source. Before it passes here it has flowed through Rhaeadr, Hay-on-Wye and Hereford and will go on to Monmouth, Tintern and the Severn estuary at Chepstow, which is my destination too.

Happy camper

Back on the river-bank, we're to make camp here. The only connection between the two banks of the river here are the two ancient hand ferries by which ferrymen, for a small fee, pull you across the river using an overhead rope. I haven't seen or heard any outboard motors or motor boats on the Wye except for two pleasure cruisers lethargically shuffling around this stretch in Symonds Yat. It's only when you get out on a river like this, that is so distant from roads and houses, that you realise how noisy life is. Our tents are flanked by willows and the quiet river. Unfortunately, the gnats and midges are hungry already and start their meal, so tomorrow we'll all be covered in red blotches.

We start early in the morning after a terrible night's sleep in the tent (possibly too many beers at the Saracen's Head). Today the camera crew in the kayak behind me want to change their position and paddle close by me to get tighter shots for our documentary. After an hour's paddling, we pass Lord's Wood, and I'm

You drive in across this bridge they've built
or sleep through the railway tunnel
or step from a shaky plane on the coast.
The roads are quite modern,
and the beer
is warm and generally flat.
The clocks keep the same time as Surbiton.

Among the ancient customs, buttering-up tourists
is not one, so beware of the remnants of pride
hanging in corners. If you prick us,
we shall surely bleed. Here you can buy
what you purchase in Selfridges
and cut a small notch in your wallet for every snip.
There are plenty of bogus Tudor
expense-account restaurants; the hotels bulge
with rugby players, their supporters still happily dissecting
a try scored in 1912.
You will feel at home in the petrol fumes.

John Tripp (1927- 1986) taken from *Welcome to Wales*

Wye valley from Wyndcliff

Jeremy Moore

*Monmouth School
rowing club*

line over his head, before plopping it into the Wye in front of me. This is one of the best rivers in Britain for salmon fishing.

I paddle past the Deer Park, Hayes Coppice and Lady Grove, where waving walkers are watching the world go by. After Fiddler's Elbow, Priory Grove and Dixton, Monmouth comes into sight. Monmouth School rowing club is taking to the water for an afternoon's sculling. I'm going to get out here, have something to eat and stretch my legs for a couple of hours.

getting into my stride. Then, in one of those moments where you wonder how on earth it could happen, I'm in the river clinging onto my kayak – the crew boat got so close that they rammed me and turned me over. The ignominy of being capsized by another kayak piloted by the crew! But apart from whacking my back on stones on the riverbed there's no damage. This is the first time that I've worn a helmet and I can see now how the most docile-looking stretch of water can suddenly become dangerous. I've lost my paddle!

I'm left on the bank with Jess, our safety instructor, who's been watching over us from a distance, and she holds my kayak to stop it floating away. We now perform a uniquely British ceremony that sees two virtual strangers pretending that one of them is not taking all his clothes off, pulling fresh ones out of plastic bags and then dressing again.

Back on the water and my lost time is quickly made up, not least because a rather alarming swan has its white wings set high and is making hissing noises very near my kayak. I pass a wading fisherman, casting his

Agincourt Square in the middle of Monmouth is dominated by the twin statues of the town's famous sons: Charles Rolls, the aviator and engineer and Henry V. Under the yellowed stone columns of the ancient Shire Hall there are flower stalls, fruit sellers and woollen goods – just as there may have been any time in the last three hundred years

Monmouth has long acted as gateway between Wales and England. A thousand years ago it was the base from which to control the troublesome Welsh districts of Archenfeld and Gwent. It was the perfect strategic position to overlook the confluence of the rivers Monnow and Wye. If trouble moved anywhere, you could watch it here.

The main street is a delight of proud shops, alleyways and a celebration of country living. The town is bustling and looks prosperous. Despite the arrival of the big multinational chains they've had to defer to Monmouth's look, rather than emblazoning their own hideous logos over their walls. This is a civilised place, rich in bookshops, art galleries and posters advertising concerts.

I've been here many times. The headmistress of Monmouth Girls School invited me to speak to the sixth form a few years back. I had prepared a talk on the media, the BBC, the licence fee, and all the predictable things I'm invited to talk about. Despite drafting and redrafting my speech I was somewhat dumbstruck at the sight of thirty doe-eyed 18-year-old girls in front of me in the lecture hall. I felt my voice seizing after the first sentence.

At the other end of Monmouth the bridge over the river Monnow is towered and ancient. It was built in 1272, but the present construction was not the first crossing. In 1988 flood prevention work unearthed the remains of an earlier bridge made of wood dating from 1140.

On the other side of the Monnow bridge you'll find St Thomas' Church, built in the 1180s. On a hot day, its cool air smelling of candle wax and polish is a welcome relief. There's a fine Norman chancel arch and an early font with an unusual design. It's all wide open to visitors and lovely.

The authors of *Camping on the Wye* came to Monmouth and went drinking in the King's Head, a seventeenth-century coaching inn frequented too by Charles I, overnighting *en route* to Raglan Castle. 'The Innkeeper in attendance had spent time in Edinburgh and was accustomed to medical students,' they report. Reading between the lines, they all got terribly drunk.

From Monmouth the Wye takes me to Tintern, where we'll camp beside the abbey. What follows first are several entrancing hours of river life: fishermen, walkers, birds, and on the banks both cattle and deer watch my

Above: Monmouth, below: statue and market on Agincourt Square

Wooded banks of the Wye

slowing progress in a long afternoon's paddle. At Redbrook, the Boat Inn hides behind a disused railway bridge, a small dinghy pulled up high on the bank before its next adventure. I am now in deep borderland: on the English side Coxbury Farm and opposite, on the Welsh side, Pentwyn Farm. Further along past Church Grove and Wyeseal Wood you'll find on the other side Pen-y-fan farm neighbouring Pwllplythin Wood.

Two hours of paddling past woodland – Penallt, Luggas Wood and Oaken Grove – and some of the most beautiful scenery yet. Further on is The Bell, where once you could ring for the boatman to ferry you across the river to the pub. Then underneath a beautiful bridge at Bigsweir I spot the toll house where the road switches allegiance from England to Wales. The Sloop Inn in Llandogo reminds you of the days when everything was transported up and down the Wye before the age of road and rail.

A few miles before Tintern, you can just see from the river the top of the signal-box at the old station. There's a platform here, signals, a water tower and waiting-room but no train service any more. A trolley laden with packing cases stands on the flagstones for a journey that will never be made. On the waiting-room wall posters advertise 'A Cheap Excursion Train on Friday 15, 1890' – that's two years before the authors of my travel guide passed by – and an excursion to the Military Exhibition in London in 1890 – 'Military Bands Daily'.

I suppose at its height the steam railway would have been both a blessing and a curse. In the 1800s nearby Chepstow was the largest port in south Wales but the arrival of the Wye Valley Railway in 1876 killed off boat traffic. The people who came to the Wye valley in those times would have had a very different view from the one I've had on my journey. The stretch of the Wye between Monmouth and Chepstow was once as well known for its industries as for its scenic beauty. Iron, copper, paper, brass: all manner of industry has been here over the centuries. Even in the 1930s picture postcards show palls of smoke over the Wye from the tinplate works. Now it's all gone, along with the trains.

The story of the decline of the Wye Valley Railway is a sad one. In post-war years the line was clearly losing money, and on Saturday, 3rd January 1959, the last scheduled service departed down the valley. That evening it snowed. Four hundred rail enthusiasts descended on the line to board a 'Special' to commemorate the last train – probably more passengers than they'd seen for decades. Later, the railway tracks were ripped up and the bridges rusted. If the Wye Valley line could have survived into the 1970s it could have blossomed as a steam tourist attraction, but it was built too early and closed too soon.

One result of the Norman conquest was the introduction of continental monasticism into Wales. The Cistercian order, the White monks, sought remote, rural locations and established a community at Tintern in 1131.

Modern visitors are impressed by the grandeur and beauty of the monastic ruins at sites such as Tintern but it is important to remember that the monks lived a hard and simple life devoted to the service of God through prayer and meditation. The surviving buildings illustrate both the daily routine of the monks and the changes made to the structure of the monastery over the four hundred years of its existence. The cloister was the hub of the monastery around which monastic life revolved; the church occupied the south side while opposite were the refectory, kitchen and dormitory; the chapter house where the monks met for their daily 'assembly' was between the parlour and the book-room on the east side of the cloister. As Tintern grew in numbers and prosperity, buildings were constructed around a second cloister north-east of the church. One of the most fascinating aspects of the site is the sophisticated drainage system which served the kitchens and the lavatories.

By the early sixteenth century monasticism was becoming unfashionable and unpopular; this helped Henry VIII in his quarrel with the Pope over the divorce from Catherine of Aragon and he persuaded parliament to close down all the monasteries between 1536 and 1540. Tintern was surrendered to royal officials in September 1536.

Unlike some of the monasteries which were transformed into country houses or parish churches, Tintern gradually became a ruin once lead had been stripped from the roof. Two hundred and fifty year later, visitors could contemplate the beauties of the river Wye, as well as the fashionable ruined abbey itself, from the boats which plied between Ross and Chepstow. Both the poet Wordsworth and the painter Turner expressed their wonderment at the tranquillity of Tintern.

Twilight at the Abbey

Back to the river, past Lyn Weir and high on the hill is a vineyard, its vines growing in straight lines up the slopes. This is Parva Farm, thought to be where the Cistercian monks of Tintern Abbey cultivated their grapes hundreds of years ago.

We are to camp tonight in the field below the abbey, our last overnight stop. Two coachloads of Japanese tourists disembark from their air-conditioned cocoon clutching cameras and race to the abbey gates to 'do' Tintern in the 30 minutes that their packed itinerary offers them here. They and I will be the last visitors of the day.

The abbey was founded in 1131 by Cistercian monks who practised a life of strict austerity, rejecting possessions and unnecessary ornament. For all that austerity, the west front of the building wouldn't disgrace a palace: it's stunningly beautiful. Despite its status as the area's top tourist attraction there is an overwhelming sense of calm and serenity here.

When the abbey was inhabited, the monk's day consisted of eight long services, the first one at 2 am. I heard recently of a television series that will follow ordinary people coping with being sent to a monastery for several months. In an age of often obscene consumerism, it seems that many of us still yearn for something that will make us happy and we're fascinated by those who have forsaken worldly goods. Were it not for women, drink and a good night's sleep I too might sign up.

When the medical students arrived in Tintern, the tide had turned and just boarding the boat to unload all their possessions was difficult. And then it started to rain: 'a cheerless drizzle . . . and darkness falling'.

'We were all soon busy staggering through mud and water unloading the boat . . . which was soon left in the sludge and reeds while Goffe as usual got the tent up, the baggage was transferred to its welcome cover, the canvas was steaming from the heat of the lamp. Under such circumstances tea is the thing.'

The two coach parties join the queue in one of the cafés for a bite to eat before their next destination. They're viewed as an inconvenience, latecomers who'll prolong the shift. It's a shame so many of the staff on the front line of British tourism seem not to enjoy taking tourists' money. I loathe the American plastic smile and the words 'Have a nice day' but so many people in our tourist industry don't seem to realise that visitors don't have to come here, and tourism is the only booming business in these parts. (By the way, if you were passing Tintern in the twilight, and saw a television crew giggling in a field trying to put up a tent, it was us after a particularly good dinner.)

A more dramatic backdrop for our camp would be difficult to imagine. And finally a thunderstorm finishes off a wonderful evening's filming. White forks light up the abbey like the opening credits of a horror film.

I wake early to the sound of cars reversing very near the tent. Dressing quickly, I look outside to find the tent is in the middle of a massive car-boot sale. The field is now full of cars and tables proudly exhibiting the unwanted detritus of Britain's attics. I'm delighted to say I've never been to a car-boot sale before, preferring to spend weekend mornings in bed with the newspapers. '78 LP records slightly damaged' it says on a cardboard sign blowing in the early-morning breeze. Broken porcelain figures and tools long since redundant lie on picnic tables. God, who buys this rubbish?

One of the stall-holders says she comes here regularly: it takes ages to load the car the night before, and they often don't sell anything, but sometimes buy from other stalls. I find myself doing what everyone else is doing, wandering around, just looking. Once we used to go to church, now we go to car-boot sales. I wonder what the monks would make of this celebration of materialism on their doorstep.

The authors of my guidebook spent their morning exploring the abbey which was full of American visitors, or Yankees as they describe them. They then visited a local farmer who produced 'his favourite ration – cyder. A handsome girl, his dark-eyed daughter bringing out a large jug of the same.' The students seem to try it on with every farmer's daughter they meet on their river

Car-boot bargains

trip down the Wye, albeit with little success. Which reminds me, this river trip will not be without a little glamour: I'm to meet Amy Guy who is Miss Wales, and also Miss UK, at Chepstow Racecourse.

This stretch of water from Tintern to Chepstow is my last. I'm genuinely sorry that with every paddle, journey's end gets ever closer. Black Morgan's Wood and Wall Weir after an hour, then the sheer cliffs of Ban-y-gor Rocks form the river-bank. The Wye bends here so tightly that it nearly forms an island. On the bank are the remains of St James Church. I leave the river just before Apostles Rocks at Walter's Weir. I've got a horse to back, a race to watch and a date with Miss Wales.

Chepstow Racecourse lies in front of Piercefield House once occupied by the sugar plantation owner Valentine Morris. His son inherited the house and spent lavishly on parties and gambling. It was later bought by Nathaniel Wells, son of a slave woman and a wealthy

Above: red-hat revolt, below: walking the course; the weighing room; Ladies' Night

plantation owner from Cardiff. Nathaniel started life as a slave, was baptised and sent to London by his father to be educated. He became one of the richest men in south Wales.

Tonight, it's Ladies Night at the races, with competitions for best hat and best-dressed lady, judged by Amy Guy. The paddock is full of racegoers in beautiful clothes and I feel singularly under-dressed. I've just realised that after hurriedly changing out of my kayaking clothes I've put on the most crumpled shirt possible, and odd socks. This won't impress Amy. The students who wrote *Camping on the Wye* had got into a similar state of scruffiness by this stage in their river journey: 'We had got into the most irregular habits; eggshells, unwashed articles thrown down anywhere and a general disinclination to amend had now settled on the whole party.'

The weighing-room at the racecourse is full of impossibly small jockeys sitting on the scales before their race, many of them having been helicoptered in after competing elsewhere today. With blackboards full of chalked names, the bookmakers are already setting up their stalls beneath the grandstand. This is a left-handed oval track, approximately two miles in circumference. At the first Welsh National held here a horse called 'Fighting Line' won with Dick Francis in the saddle. Now I wonder whatever happened to him?

The first race today is for three-year-old horses over one mile. There are only seconds left to place a bet – I put £10 on a horse called 'In Deep' in memory of my Wye journey. I have no idea if it's a good prospect, but the bookie in a trilby exchanges my note for a wry smile and a receipt. As numbers swell by the hundreds every minute, thousands of people at once look in one direction to the race start, and then begins a continuous deafening shout of different horses' names. 'Yes! Arthur's Dream!', 'Come on, Public Eye!' After only a few seconds this climaxes in a mixture of hysterical cheers and a deep groan, including mine.

The next race is the Novice Stakes for two-year-old horses. The shouts begin again but I have no idea who wins, and care even less, because at that moment Miss Wales, alias Amy Guy, arrives next to us and we all spend the rest of the race trying to chat her up. I can see why the judges thought she was the most beautiful woman not only in Wales but the UK, and she also happens to be witty and intelligent. She is dreading having to choose a winner later from among the beautiful women of Chepstow who have dressed up for Ladies Night.

In the way that life imitates art, just as the medical students completed their Wye river journey without taking on any extra female passengers, we too quickly discover our fate. Cameraman, soundman, director and yours truly all look on in rapture while Amy tells us of her plans to practise architecture when her time as Miss UK comes to an end, and then, that wounding moment, the discussion turns to her interesting boyfriend in London. Grown men flinch. So, Amy doesn't find her new, scruffy, sweating, stubbled and damp companions attractive after all. Ah, well.

The last few days on the Wye have been a wonderful journey for all that, and I hope to remember the calm of the river for a long time to come.

Above: a race to the finish
below: tranquil waters

Five years have passed; five summers, with the length
Of five long winters! and again I hear
These waters, rolling from their mountain-springs
With a sweet inland murmur. – Once again
Do I behold these steep and lofty cliffs,
Which on a wild secluded scene impress
Thoughts of more deep seclusion; and connect
The landscape with the quiet of the sky.

Oh! how oft,
In darkness, and amid the many shapes
Of joyless day-light; when the fretful stir
Unprofitable, and the fever of the world,
Have hung upon the beatings of my heart,
How oft, in spirit, have I turned to thee
O sylvan Wye! Thou wanderer through the woods,
How often has my spirit turned to thee!

William Wordsworth (1770-1850)
from 'Lines written a few miles above Tintern Abbey'

Tintern

Martin Cavaney

ON THE WRITER'S
TRAIL

THE BRECON BEA

MANOEUVRES AND MEMORIES

Aled Hughes

I'm following roughly the route of the old Roman road from Aberdulais towards Brecon, marked on the map as Sarn Helen. I've never been to Aberdulais, the place that Turner painted and

CONS

Cordell wrote about, so I'll begin my exploration of the Neath valley at Aberdulais Falls. As for the end of this journey, I spent seven years at school in Brecon, so a return journey beckons.

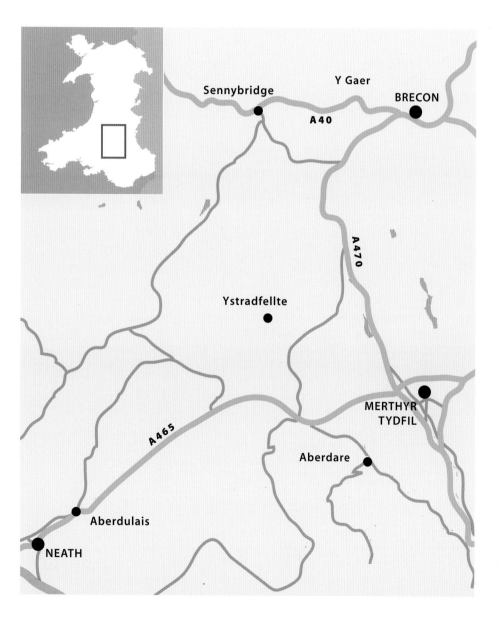

YOU'LL FIND THE FALLS TUCKED BESIDE the busy main road that leads from the M4 up the Neath valley. The water from the river Neath has been harnessed over at least four centuries and possibly as far back as Roman times in order to power copper-smelting, corn-grinding and tinplate-making. Now the falls are a tourist attraction, beautiful ruins of industrial buildings made of stone, roofless now and lying quiet and empty, framed by a canopy of oak trees in full leaf. In the centre is Europe's biggest working waterwheel, generating enough hydro-electricity to power two thousand televisions. Its sloshing hum is an almost musical accompaniment to a wander around.

Looking at the industrial heritage of Wales, I often feel in awe of its visionary architects. I admire, too, the sheer determination that must have been required for such enormous feats of engineering. Can you imagine the conversation in the pub in rural Wales just before the canals were built, or before railway tracks and tunnels were laid? In an age before consultation and universal suffrage, whole villages were moved, land seized, and farms cut up with extraordinary speed. Can you imagine somebody suggesting these kinds of schemes today? There would be years of meetings and then somebody in a committee would be called on to write a report. Brunel would have shot himself waiting for planning permission. Not that the development at Aberdulais was without its outspoken critics in the nineteenth century.

The gorge and falls as we see them today are not quite what Nature created: they were altered considerably by quarrying. So much so that in 1820,

Capt R.H. Gronow recorded his disgust at this 'act of vandalism'.

'A natural cascade called Dyllais was destroyed by an agent to Lord Jersey in order to build a few cottages and the lock of a canal. The rock down which this beautiful cascade had flowed from the time of the flood and which had created a scene of beauty universally admired was blown up with gunpowder by this man.' Disgusted of Aberdulais.

And now, interestingly, we come to admire that act of vandalism.

In its heyday this was probably a complete hellhole of dangerous working conditions, long hours and dreadful pay but, after a century of dereliction, the smell and noise of manufacturing have gone and what is left is a perfect romantic relic of Welsh manufacturing. I wonder if the National Trust will one day give guided tours of our oil refineries, nuclear power stations and wind farms. Will anyone feel sentimental about them?

If the custodians of historical attractions were to attempt to recreate the original odour of properties in its custody, this place would honk of hot metal, coal and steam. There would be smoke, too, and clouds of steam. The painter J.M.W. Turner must have seen something of that when he came here in 1795 and painted Aberdulais Falls and again the following year to capture Aberdulais Mill. I hope he found a place to park.

The earliest known use of water power here was in 1584 when a copper-smelting works was established; water would have powered bellows to provide air for open furnaces where copper ore was roasted. By 1631 a corn mill was operating near the waterfall, the mill being powered by an overshot waterwheel. Twenty years later, the trade was in woollen cloth – softened by

Aberdulais

Banwen race-track;
pit-stop; wrong turn

today. The only smell is of freshly-cut grass clippings carpeting the floors of the ruined buildings. Heron, dippers and kingfishers feed on fat fish and insects skim the clear water of the Dulais which rises near Onllwyn in the Brecon Beacons some eight miles away. Salmon and sea trout are visitors here, swimming past the shadows of the ruins. They spend most of their time in the sea but return to spawn up river. During November, salmon lay their eggs in the gravel of the riverbed, then once the eggs hatch and the fish have grown, the adults make for the sea. They cross the Atlantic and travel to the coast of Greenland – a seven-thousand-mile round trip. It's a prospect so exhausting that I must have some tea and cake.

If you've never been to a National Trust tearoom staffed by volunteers then you really must seek one out. Aberdulais Falls tearoom is a temple to tea and cake. Sandwiches, tea, *bara brith* and Welsh cakes all flow for as long as I continue to make delighted noises.

'I really shouldn't, but if you made it this morning and will take offence at refusal, then perhaps I'll just have another small slice.'

The volunteers say that most of their visitors are from outside Wales and that local people don't take much interest in the place. It was hard to say goodbye, but I knew that one more piece of cake and my stomach would explode – which would be messy in a National Trust property. Just think of the paperwork.

Sarn Helen passes Neath, Melincourt, Resolven, Pentreclwydau, Blaen-gwrach and Seven Sisters as it makes its way through this historic valley. This was once big coal-mining country but now many mines are

a pounding process called fulling in use here in 1653, and by 1667 a dyeing house had been built. Finally, and perhaps best-known in this area, a tinplate works powered by water and steam opened in 1832; the rolling mills reduced wrought iron bar into thin sheets for tinning. By the 1880s the works had closed.

I probably would have found little to enjoy had I visited Aberdulais when it was a place of work. It would be like having a day out to visit a car factory. Shifts at the tinplate works were usually 12 hours a day, six days a week. Although the workers knew nothing else, it must have been a hard life with small rewards. And it wasn't just men working here: women and children were employed at the works to separate, stack and polish tin plates.

The silent ivy-clad ruins of the tinplate works today give no inkling of the nineteenth-century spectacle of smoking chimneys and human toil. The burning heat of the tin platers' fires has long gone. The air is sweet museums. At Banwen, where there was once a massive opencast mine, the search for a new lease of life has delivered motor racing in the shape of Walters Arena. Where they once dug millions of tons from the mountains at Maes-gwyn quarry, they have reshaped the hills once again to provide hair-raising thrills for the world's rally drivers testing their cars. The Wales Rally GB is hosted here.

When we arrive, they're racing three-wheeled Reliant Robins at breakneck speed as a warm-up to amuse the crowds before the main event. I've never understood the thrill of motor racing, but up close to the mud, flaming brakes and screeching engines I can now see the attraction. The spectators are local men, some women and lots of children loving every minute of it. This is such a massive expanse of open land that it's ideal to test cars and their components to destruction.

In one of those slow-motion moments you see in the movies, the proper racing begins and a Ford rally car literally flies over the brow of a hill, spraying gravel everywhere; it turns over twice and lands upside down. Showing my inexperience in motor racing, I hear myself gasp in horror whilst the seasoned spectators slowly wander down to the track and help right the car onto its wheels. These vehicles are meant to be rolled and crashed.

Most of the cars we drive on the roads are safer because of the kind of engineering and testing that takes place in sessions like this one, apparently.

And the world's manufacturers are all coming here to the middle of Wales – the people of Banwen are getting used to helicopters dropping off motor-sport

Just a scratch

celebrities. Who would have thought that the glory days of coal would be replaced by world motor sport as a burgeoning new industry? I leave feeling uplifted that there is something keeping people in skilled jobs in this community.

Within a few miles, the small villages clinging to the roadway give way to wider skies and shallower slopes; an old industrial landscape is replaced by hill farms, whitewashed farmyards, rusting tractors and ancient Landrovers. It's quiet and it's lunchtime.

Heading beyond Ystradfellte, the road stops suddenly before taking a deep breath, closing its eyes and zig-zagging like an alpine pass to the bottom of the valley. There are few better views to enjoy while having your lunch; it's jaw-droppingly beautiful, a magnificent vista over a thousand green and yellow fields to Sennybridge on the horizon. I'm sitting at the meeting place of dozens of dry-stone walls, which must have taken a lifetime to gather and build. It's silent, except for the incessant grass-munching of hundreds of sheep.

Through the lock now into a golden land where coo-pidges were wimpering and willows weeping and the bright cut winding through a country of honey and milk and great swathes of green over the glorious mountains . . . the tinplate workers from the works above Aberdulais on the Nedd gave a welcome, strangers or not, straight from the Dandy-fires, their cheeks patched red with the heat, they clustered in their white smocks, the melters, picklers, tinners and branders and waved and shouted, and Gran lined up with Sharon and Gwen and went down in curtseys while we got up and bowed, for there is nothing the Welsh like better than good manners.

Alexander Cordell from *Song of the Earth*

Martin Cavaney

THE EPYNT: A VANISHED COMMUNITY

Jeremy Moore

Ironically, a fake village has been created on the range for training purposes. It does not resemble any of the settlements that were lost.

Thousands of ex-soldiers who trained at Sennybridge camp will know the Epynt ranges well, though probably not as well as the people who once lived in this beautiful area. In 1940 the government requisitioned thousands of acres of land here for military purposes and over two hundred people were forced to leave their fifty-four homes. This sudden destruction of a remote, rural, Welsh community provoked vigorous opposition from nationalists such as Saunders Lewis and Gwynfor Evans but for most people the exigencies of war justified this dramatic act.

Although the Epynt is a remote, upland area the inhabitants had regular contacts with the villages and small towns on the periphery. Garth, Llangammarch Wells, Merthyr Cynog, Upper Chapel and Sennybridge offered markets, horse fairs, eisteddfodau and professional services such as doctors. However, much of their social life centred on the three hubs of the Epynt community – the chapel (Y Babell), the school in Cwm Cilieni and the Drovers' Arms.

A moving account of life on the Epynt before the brutal clearance can be found in *An Uprooted Community* by Herbert Hughes. He described a society largely unaffected by what we take for granted: people and children walked, to chapel and to school; horses provided the pulling power on the farms; Welsh was the language of the heart but English ruled at school; folk remedies – for both humans and animals – meant that doctors and vets were only consulted in emergencies; families helped and supported each other in times of need and celebration.

In 1940 Iorwerth Peate the founder of the Museum of Welsh Life at St Fagans visited the Epynt to survey and photograph the houses which were being emptied. He met an old lady who had been born on the Epynt and she urged Peate to return to Cardiff, 'My dear boy, go back there as soon as you can, it is the end of the world here.'

Then a mile above me, the blast from a jet breaks the spell like a stone thrown into still water.

I think this is one of my favourite views – I now find myself sitting in the car drawing up my list of the top ten best views in Wales and then arguing with my shortlist. (Mustn't stay here too long in case I need medical assistance.) In the space of just a few miles both landscape and the lives lived here change dramatically. The farmers and their families who live up here inhabit a completely different country from those who live in the valley I've just left behind. Their horizons look different, their experience is different and their interpretation of Wales and being Welsh is, I think, wholly different.

I'm not entirely sure myself what the term Welsh or Wales means other than its administrative use; certainly the people of Aberdulais and the south Wales valleys have a completely different take on what it means compared to the farmers of the Brecon Beacons. I think we are a nation of disparate tribes, with little that binds us together – save the rain. Hills like these on either side of me don't bring people together, they keep them apart. And with that deep and meaningless bombshell, it's time to retrace my steps and drive down valley to Blaen Llia.

Arwel Michael has walked the Brecon Beacons all of his life and we're to interview him on one of his favourite walks which happens to be along Sarn Helen. He's waiting for us at the car park which the Romans thoughtfully provided at the side of their road. We walk for a few miles to a standing stone thought to mark an

Senni valley; Maen Llia standing stone; Sennybridge ranges

Dyfed Elis-Gruffydd

Operation Bardic Strike, Sennybridge

ancient grave. No sooner do we start filming the interview than a convoy of a dozen off-road vehicles from a Midlands 4 x 4 club drive along the Roman road we've just walked. Nothing wrong with that except for the fact that they don't stick to the road. The lead vehicle lurches off-road into a deep mud pool which obviously has regular weekend use, and is slowly undermining the Roman construction. I guess if the Romans had left an amphitheatre or coliseum on this spot, then it would be lovingly maintained and protected, but in a country with a crowded ancient history we allow the vandalism of a relic as old as Christianity simply because we have a lot of relics. I know there's a fine line between encouraging leisure in the countryside and protecting heritage but a bunch of petrol heads from Wolverhampton are tearing history to pieces for heaven's sake! Must take blood pressure tablets.

A few miles to the north where Mynydd Epynt towers above Crychan Forest, the army is holding a massive military exercise on Sennybridge ranges. The mountain road is lined with green, three-ton army trucks, ambulances, police cars and, later, two helicopters. As one of the country's top training arenas for British soldiers, this landscape over the years has played the part of France, Germany, the Falkland Islands and Iraq. Today, the exercise supposes that the United Kingdom has experienced days of continuous torrential rain and flooding. (If you're Welsh, this bit will be easy to visualise.) Heavy rain combined with extraordinary high tides has caused devastation throughout the country. Hundreds of soldiers are involved in exercise Operation

Bardic Strike. The exercise is centred on civil contingency and has been designed to test call-out procedures that would be followed in the event of major disaster.

It has never occurred to me that the army rehearses assistance for the emergency services. Yet I'm always struck by the extraordinary quality of the men and women who make up the British services. They are a breed apart. Many of the soldiers are territorials who hold down day jobs but drop everything to get soaked in the name of service – so that should disaster strike they will simply get on with the job as they always do, without complaint or question. It's humbling watching them train for hours how to drop out of helicopters, search for missing plastic children and bring order to the imagined chaos of blocked roads and washed-away bridges. I'll sleep easier in my bed having seen them in action.

The road to Brecon follows the river Usk past Trallong, Aberysgir and Llanspyddid. It's warming up nicely as I approach the town. Brecon is one of those places you can walk around in an hour and you will be constantly delighted. The cathedral is a most beautiful building, modest and human in scale, more large parish church than diocesan headquarters. We've arranged with John Davies, the Dean, to go up to the top of the cathedral tower to film high shots of the town. It's a narrow and sometimes claustrophobic squash climbing with our filming gear along narrow passages, but the reward at the top after hundreds of worn, dusty steps leaves us all quiet for a moment.

A few hundred feet beneath us the pattern of streets is spread like an ancient tapestry: the medieval bending

From Brecon cathedral tower

Brecon Cathedral

lines of the Struet's tumbling pastel houses, the remains of the castle, the Watton, Free Street, Lion Street and, beneath the backdrop of the hills, Christ College's monastic buildings. The rivers Usk and Honddu meet here – a confluence that gives the town its Welsh name, Aberhonddu. It all looks small and close enough to scoop up in my hands.

Filming done, we gingerly descend the narrow steps built for smaller feet, before the bells strike the hour and deafen us.

The camera crew wander off for coffee so I have a few minutes inside the cathedral. The prayer requests book is open for visitors. Written in a young hand in biro: 'Dear Lord, sorry for all the times I have betrayed you. Rhys.'

Another entry: 'Pray for my Dad who died – we miss him so much. Julia.'

Further down the page: 'For my daughter Sarah, born and died the same day.' Unsigned.

I feel a wave of sorrow thinking of those who have stood here to write. In a society of the television confessional, the unspoken words of the silent visitors to this place of worship seem so dignified and old-fashioned. The faithful have been walking beneath these stone arches for nine hundred years to seek solace in a troubled world. I hope those who wrote here today found it. The last entry of the mother who lost her baby stays in my mind for the rest of our time in Brecon.

I came to the cathedral as a twelve-year-old boy soprano rehearsing for the BBC's *Songs of Praise* from Brecon. I remember being entranced by the splendour of the place and the beauty of the music. There was an orchestra here and every choir in the county was taking part. Many years later I stepped in to present *Songs of Praise* for the BBC for a couple of programmes but I kept my earlier musical appearance on the programme quiet, lest they found embarrassing archive footage.

An undertaker opens the main door carrying a wreath, and walks the length of the cathedral to a flag-draped coffin. I leave before the mourners arrive, suddenly feeling an intruder on private grief.

I always feel a sense of naughtiness walking through the streets of Brecon. For a boarding-school pupil, time 'up town' as it was known, was strictly rationed and timetabled. Walking around the town was viewed as a privilege that increased in hours as the school years passed. In the first year we were allowed to go to Brecon for an hour on Tuesday afternoons; just enough time for an eleven-year-old to gaze at matchbox cars or train sets. As we grew older, the destinations changed to cafés, the illicit back bar of the Wellington, Brecon Corinthians Sports Club and the convent school. Going 'up town' also allowed us to stock up on hot pies to supplement the school food.

On market days Brecon used to be dominated by farmers, their trailers and cattle, but the cattle market has been moved out of town now to make way for a supermarket. The town is still the genteel, attractive, easy-going place that I've always loved. Life moves more slowly here, and you have to build in time to talk to people you'll meet in the streets. When you've spent too long living in cities you forget that people who live in small towns and villages aren't in the manic hurry that urban dwellers are. Brecon is better for that.

Above: The Struet
below: Bridge over the Usk at Brecon

ROMAN ACTIVITY

Aled Hughes

Roman Wales was a military zone and it is only to be expected that the surviving remains are largely the work of soldiers – marching camps, forts and, most notably, roads.

Dotted across Ordnance Survey maps are the words Sarn Helen – examples can be seen near the Roman fort at Coelbren and again on Mynydd Illtud, near Brecon. Sarn is Welsh for road and Helen was reputedly the Welsh wife of Magnus Maximus (Macsen Wledig in Welsh) a Spanish general who declared himself Emperor while serving in Britain.

While they fought to subdue the native Silures the soldiers built a number of temporary marching camps, two of which can be seen as earthworks on the moorland above Trecastle. But

the most notable Roman site in the area – and one which deserves to be much better known – is at Y Gaer, three miles west of Brecon. The fort was originally excavated in the 1920s by Sir Mortimer

Wheeler, who apparently enjoyed the salmon fishing in the Usk, and much of what he uncovered can still be seen. The perimeter wall on the north side stands over six feet high in places and the foundations of the west gate give a good idea of the sophisticated building work done by the legionaries. Some of the finds from Y Gaer are displayed in the Brecknock Museum & Art Gallery. In addition to the usual pieces of Samian ware there are two remarkable tombstones: the first, the so-called Maen y Morwynion (the Maidens' Stone) shows a man and his wife holding hands, the second has an inscription which tells us the man commemorated was a member of a Spanish cavalry regiment. The international nature of the Empire is made very real when one looks at this memorial to a dead Spaniard serving Rome on the Welsh frontier.

Aled Hughes

Down Ship Street to the Watergate and across the bridge over the Usk to Llanfaes. I always feel a sense of mixed emotions coming back to Christ College. This boarding school was home for seven years. In many respects I am what this place made me – good and bad. I first came here as a rather shy eleven-year-old boy with no great talent and large quantities of indolence. I was small and skinny for my age in a school of impossibly tall, confident people. My birthday cake was in a tin in a trunk full of clothes on which my mother and grandmother had spent the summer sewing my name and my school number. I was to get used to being known as Owen for the next few years: Christian names were not used until much later.

Unlike many children sent away to school, I had been given the choice to go. This was a cunning move on the part of my parents. When, later, the going got difficult, I reminded myself it was my choice to be there. I hadn't been sent away by my parents.

Leaving Mum and Dad behind was cleverly blurred by a tea party where new boys and their parents got to know each other in the ancient dining-room. My parents slipped away so that none of us had to endure the sight of tears. I felt an extraordinary sense of contradictory emotions that would stay with me for the rest of my days there. I was alone and yet forced to spend the coming years with little privacy. I missed my family, the dog and Pembrokeshire's coast but at the same time felt an extraordinary sense of privilege to be part of this achingly beautiful ancient school at the foot of the Beacons. That sense of conflicting emotions would manifest itself in a mixture of nervousness and car-sickness every time I left home for a new term. Even

Class of 1979

as I write this so many years later, I can feel that knot in my stomach that would develop as we got into the car.

Home for me for the next year was a dormitory shared with twenty other boys, my belongings were stored in a cupboard-sized wardrobe and my bed had a concave mattress (there was always a race back at the start of term to swap a duff one). Every hour of every day was timetabled. I remember the shock of discovering there were lessons on a Saturday and timetabled slots for games, homework and even model-airplane-making. Idle boys were a danger to themselves and to be occupied at all times.

The housemaster of Alway House, the junior house at Christ College, was Colin Kleiser – a Francophile and a cricket-mad disciplinarian. He ruled the sixty children in his charge with a rod of iron. In the first year, a variety of ancient gouty old boys returned to address the new pupils. Robert Ackerman had just distinguished himself playing rugby for Wales and the Liberal Democrat MP Simon Hughes won a famous by-election victory at Bermondsey. I don't ever recall a word on the subject of ambition in all my time there but

Christ College, Brecon

the ancient photographs on the walls, the chapel plaques remembering those who'd served the Empire, and an acknowledgement of over four hundred years of history – all of these pointed somehow to an expectation of success. It was success in duty, though, that was celebrated, not material wealth: that tended to be treated with disdain. Achievers in the armed services, the church, in education or in the community were the guiding lights to steer by.

My new school friends were the children of farmers, lawyers, car dealers, doctors and the local Chinese takeaway owner. For many, sending their son here meant a clear choice to skip on the big house, luxury car and foreign holidays: many families were making a substantial financial sacrifice for their children's education. This was not the alma mater of landed gentry or city financiers, but simply where some of the Welsh middle classes of south Wales sent their children.

Christ College was in those days a single-sex institution until the sixth form. That fact, coupled with Christ College being one of the country's top rugby schools, meant that there was in those days a sense of

physical brutality about it. Masters, often in academic gowns, could be inspiring or terrifying. Christopher Potter tried unsuccessfully to teach me maths, although we were not to discover common ground until I helped him change the brakepads on his elderly Rover. Colin Kleiser used a substantial Larousse dictionary to knock French into our heads. Gareth Jones taught us to love English and my history teacher, Edward Parry, is still correcting my essays. Clive Burn, the conductor of the chapel choir, instilled in me a lifelong love of sacred music, although that sometimes competed with my interest in drama. They were not the tendencies that were most revered in an institution that was in those days so inclined towards sporting prowess.

It's as well our parents were a long way away – they couldn't see our crossings of the almost-freezing, flooded river in January, in PE kit of course, with former SAS soldier Mike Owens yelling orders. Mid-stream we encountered a dead sheep floating towards us and, in the way that adversity characterises schoolboy humour, I remember us, chest-deep, debating whether the animal had frozen to death in January weather or committed suicide to avoid February.

The banter and repartee began early. It was how, if you weren't big enough or tough enough, you stayed out of trouble. Classes were small so there was nowhere to hide – make 'em laugh before they make you cry. It was good training for all those who'd later have to stand up in court and think on their feet either as lawyers or defendants. Those who say they survived prison or kidnapping because they went to a British boarding school are telling the truth – what was missing from our term was the crime. Punishments were harsh and sometimes fair. On one occasion I was delivered back to school after a weekend and walked into the house roll-call as the Williams names were being called, so missing the Owens by minutes. My punishment for being late was 60 lines or two whacks of the slipper, which I opted for because it was quicker. I think Christ College believed that preparing children for life meant readying them for the odd injustice too. Since then I've been a fanatical timekeeper – so remember that if you invite me out for a drink.

The setting for education couldn't have been more perfect. Sport was played, albeit reluctantly by me, on beautiful playing fields surrounded by mountains. Walking to breakfast we passed ancient monastic buildings, and choir practice took place in a thirteenth-century chapel that looked like a film set. It was easy to write descriptively when the view out of the window was a work of art.

I think boarding school inevitably changes the nature of your relationships with your family. My two younger brothers refused to go away to school, and we spent the best part of our teenage years apart, which they tell me was a good thing. My parents and grandmother wrote to me religiously every week. My father would always scribble on second-hand lawyer's correspondence – reams detailing the goings-on of our family, his staff and news of the dog, who would sometimes co-sign his letters.

My friends who didn't go to boarding school are sometimes appalled to hear that they still exist and for my part I still can't decide if I'd send my children away

Christ College

to school if they wanted to go. There is inevitably a trade-off between the wonderful and rounded opportunities the experience offers and the hurt caused by removing a child from family life at the age of eleven or twelve. Even those who love me say I'm too emotionally self-contained, infuriatingly self-sufficient, that I work too hard and am incapable of switching off. All are possibly the attributes that I developed to survive Christ College. For all that, I know that without this place I'd be stacking shelves somewhere. The day I left, seven years later, I was reduced to tears. I loved the school but it's a strange kind of love – which defies satisfactory explanation to this day.

The chapel, library, School House and weeping willow, surrounded by immaculate lawns, look as beautiful today as they did the day I arrived in 1979.

David Emrys James
(Dewi Emrys)
trans. Tony Conran

HORIZON

Look, a mirage, like a round rim, a strange
Wizard's masterpiece about us:
An old line that's not there,
A boundary that never ends.

Maen Llia

Aled Hughes

Y GORWEL

Wele rith fel ymyl rhod – o'n cwmpas,
    Campwaith dewin hynod;
    Hen linell bell nad yw'n bod,
    Hen derfyn nad yw'n darfod.

SNOWDON

A SUMMIT IN SUNSHINE

One of our first family holidays was in Snowdonia. My parents, my brothers Huw and Richard and I – together with a week's luggage – were all squeezed into a wheezing Mini 1000 with which my father set out to do battle with the hills. We stayed in a log cabin in the foothills of Snowdonia, next to a farm. And for three small boys it was paradise found.

Steve Lewis

Moel Siabod on a winter dawn

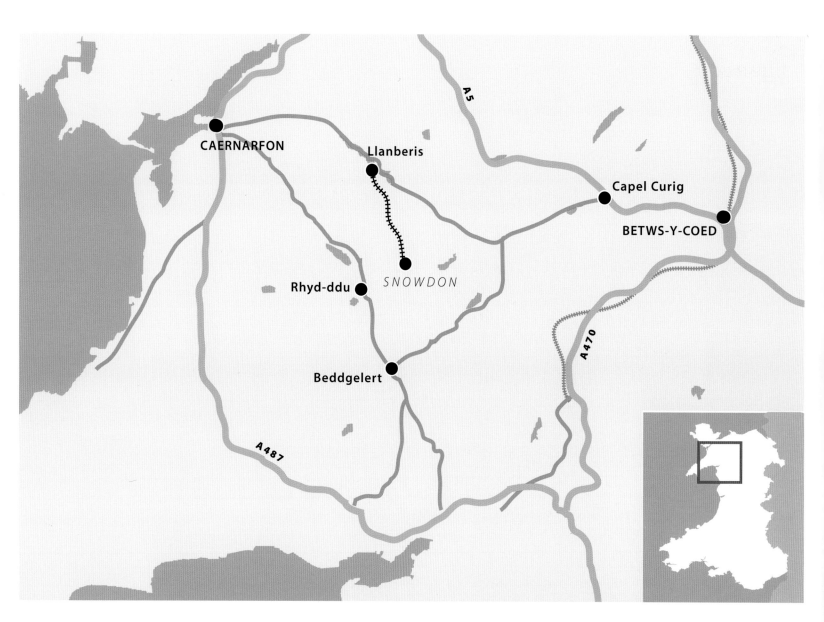

SNOWDON

Snowdonia ruin

DAD DIDN'T LIKE HOLIDAYS MUCH; HE'D travelled the world with the army for years and would have been quite happy to spend the rest of his life at home. It was my mother who wrenched her workaholic husband off for a week's holiday here or there. I remember the long journey from Pembrokeshire to Snowdonia as much as the holiday itself. The dark green valleys, waterfalls, a puppet show, unfamiliar place-names, fish fingers – and the pleasure of travel for its own sake. That it was also one of the hottest summers in years engraves that holiday on our collective memory. Bizarrely, we never got to climb Snowdon itself. I don't know if it was the lure of the farm or the problem of having one very small child in tow that kept us away, or that my parents' map reading let them down! That was thirty years ago.

My journey just to get to Snowdonia on a bank holiday Friday takes me the best part of four hours. It's late afternoon, and the water in the rivers Severn, Ieithon and Wye at the side of the road are low, since it hasn't rained for days. Brecon, Builth and Rhaeadr are filling up slowly with visitors escaping the city for a long weekend in Wales. Then I come to Llangurig – nearly half way now – and, after a few hours, Machynlleth and Dolgellau, two historic towns with magnificent Cadair Idris between them. Plenty of inspiration here for another Welsh journey another day.

Our plan this time is to climb Snowdon and meet the people who live and work on the mountain. The weather is always changeable here, but over the next four days we hope to have two perfect days for filming. Climbing Snowdon is daunting enough if you've never done it before, but in order to capture the journey for television, we will have to carry our equipment with us: tripod, sound-recording gear, camera and dozens of blank videotapes – as well as the usual paraphernalia of waterproofs, food and drink that anyone would take on a day on the mountain.

The pub benches of Betws-y-coed are full of weekend climbers, many of them staying in the campsite across the main road, which looks like a shanty town of canvas. I'm grateful that on this adventure I won't be camping: the sky looks threatening and I don't fancy climbing Snowdon soaked and tired. We're all to stay at the Royal Oak tonight where the Moelwyn Male Voice Choir is singing as I check in. The visitors eating and drinking there obviously love the music – either that or they're too drunk to escape.

Though travellers have been coming here for centuries, Betws-y-coed wasn't really on the tourist trail until 1808 when road improvements put the town on the mail coach route. Better roads meant people could

Betws-y-coed

visit more quickly to explore the natural attractions, and when artists like Turner came here and his paintings became known, it encouraged more visitors. By the time of the Victorians and their railways in 1868, the town was a bustling tourist destination and a base-camp for walking in Snowdonia. .

Glen Evans, who has taken over the hotel from his parents, heaves an old hotel registration book onto his counter. It's full of entries from the 1890s of visitors from Canada, Pennsylvania, Texas and Washington. Imagine any one of those journeys to come here before the age of aeroplanes: an adventure of epic proportions. Suddenly my four-hour drive across the length of Wales seems rather insignificant. The visitors here tonight are mostly from Liverpool and Manchester.

Betws-y-coed is north Wales's most popular inland resort, the meeting place of the rivers Conwy, Llugwy, Lledr and Machno. If cascading waterfalls, hilltop lakes and ancient bridges are your thing, then this place is for you. An artist colony of sorts grew up here in the late nineteenth century when the area was discovered by the landscape artist David Cox. He and the Liverpool artist Clarence Whaite were influential in making the area better known.

Before dinner I set out to explore for an hour or so. I'm glad it's not raining now, but I know that bad weather is the best time to see Pont-y-pair (the bridge of the cauldron), built in 1468, which is spectacular when the river is full of foaming water after heavy rain. The pavements are full of walkers back from visiting Fairy Glen and Thomas Telford's Waterloo Bridge built in 1815 to cross the river Conwy.

The sun sets early behind the green wooded hills high above Betws-y-coed. The television crew have all travelled from different directions and different assignments, so we meet over a beer to discuss plans for the coming days. In the beer garden, a man dressed as a native American Indian staggers from table to table with a fuel can asking for money to buy petrol for his stranded vehicle a few miles away. Chris, our director, gives him a pound, but by the time he leaves he's collected enough money to buy a new car.

The midges seem to like drinking in the open air as much as we do, and before long their bites send us inside. We need a good night's sleep before climbing Snowdon tomorrow.

At first light, Snowdonia is waking to a more brutal day. Betws-y-coed has turned into Kagool City, and last night's campers waddle around squelching awkwardly in damp clothes, searching the streets for a hot shower and a cooked breakfast. The mood is subdued over breakfast: our television programme will be pretty dismal without sunshine. Yesterday's beautiful countryside has degenerated into a formidable and menacing landscape.

We drive past Llynnau Mymbyr to Pen-y-pas above Nant Gwynant to have a coffee with Sam Roberts, one of the most experienced wardens in the Snowdonia National Park. He'll be more accurate than the national weather forecast and we'll take his advice on whether to proceed with our filming of Snowdon. Through the windscreen of the Landrover, this is shaping up to be a pretty gruesome day. Sam has spent his life walking in these mountains and has worked as a warden here for 30

Above: Betws-y-coed, below: Llynnau Mymbyr and Snowdon

Steve Lewis

Nant Ffrancon

years. This morning Pen-y-pas is full of hundreds of waterproofed walkers, young and old, soaking wet and steaming in the dry warm of the teashop before venturing out into the cold again. Sam sits in his warden's office – he's seen it all before, and like a wise old bird takes down the latest satellite radar weather forecasts that sound the death knell for our climb up Snowdon today. 'Best to have a cup of tea and try again tomorrow,' he says. So that's what we do: our meticulously-planned filming schedule which was to include aerial shots from the helicopter has been scuppered by the weather.

We decide to make for Cwm Idwal, which might be sheltered enough for us to film with the National Park ranger Alan Pritchard. Alan was a shepherd who worked these slopes for many years before turning his attention to the tourist flock. He's evangelical about showing the ice-age gouging of the rock, so we don boots for the first time and set out. I'm trying not to breathe too heavily beside Alan as he sets a breakneck speed. I'm beginning to realise how unfit I am.

But we won't be walking more than a few miles this afternoon. The rain stops for an hour only to be replaced with winds strong enough to rip off car doors.

Cwm Idwal is one of the best places in Britain to learn about geology. Admittedly it's colder and wetter than your average classroom, but so much less dull. It came into being some 400 million years ago, the result of the crushing and folding of rocks – the product of earlier violent volcanic eruptions – when two ancient continents clashed and formed these mountains. A huge glacier flowed out of the basin where Llyn Idwal now

The faces of Tryfan

rests, scratching the rocks beneath as it began its downward journey along what is now the Nant Ffrancon valley. The rest of Alan's fascinating natural history lecture is lost on me, as I take the opportunity while we stop and look to catch my breath. Goodness knows how I'll cope with climbing four or five hours up Snowdon tomorrow. The diet and abstinence from wine start tonight.

Charles Darwin came here to Cwm Idwal and famously failed to notice all the evidence of glaciation all around him. He later wrote: 'We did not notice the plainly scored rocks, the perched boulders, the lateral and terminal moraines. Yet these phenomena are so conspicuous that a house burnt down by fire did not tell its story more plainly than did this valley.'

Don't be so hard on yourself, Charles, I completely understand. (He was probably holding onto the rocks for dear life – no wonder he missed the signs of glaciation). Alan points out Tryfan in the mist: 'If you cock your head it looks like a human face. I think it looks a bit like Queen Victoria, or a Red Indian Chief', he says.

I try hard to visualise both faces but decide not to tell him that all I can see is Homer Simpson.

There is something missing here and it takes a while for me to work out what it is. Then it dawns on me: there are no sheep. It's the only time I've been in upland Wales without the accompaniment of bleating, but sheep are not welcome here. Lambs are removed from

Steve Lewis

Llyn Idwál and Pen yr Ole Wen

the valley to encourage flowering plants and grasses in an attempt to understand the flora and fauna of the region before extensive grazing. The rocks are volcanic which provide arctic-alpine plants with the nutrients they need to flourish, so crags and crevices reveal real treasures, some of them having hung on since the ice age. (There are a few people like that at the BBC.) These plants need cold conditions and some need little sun, so they'll be delirious today. On the ledges beyond the reach of man (should you be mad enough to crawl to look), you'll see moss campion, mountain avens, Welsh poppy, alpine lady's mantle and purple saxifrage. At least I think that's what Alan shouted above the howling gale – though he could just as well have yelled, 'Hurry up, fat boy, you're holding us up.'

The wind is now so strong we cannot continue filming without hiding behind the rocks scattered like large toys. A party of stooped students walk down the slope with a speed prompted by the knowledge that they're not far from the warmth of their bus, but clearly they're exhausted by a day in the mountains. Then, as we take a breather from carrying camera gear, a cry comes from a student lifted right off his feet and dumped yards away by a terrifying gust of wind. There's no damage done, and he walks off bewildered and relieved, his friends who have run back to help now leading him safely away.

This has been a sobering few hours. The sunny playground of the picture postcards has gone, to be replaced by a rather discomforting place.

After what seems like an age, but only because the headwind slows our walking, we reach the shores of the magnificent Llyn Idwal. It lies in the shadow of Devil's Kitchen and right now the devil himself might be pounding its surface. We crouch at its side rather like you would hide from a couple arguing furiously. In this atrocious wind, I can't imagine a better day to see it in all its spitting hostility.

Tonight we are to spend the evening in the Pen-y-Gwryd Hotel, the hallowed watering-hole for mountaineers. This is the hotel climbers have used as base-camp for climbing Snowdon as a preparation for conquering peaks around the world. The Everest expedition team stayed here before their successful ascent in 1953. If you didn't know before about the part this place played in the history of world mountaineering, you need only to walk through the front door to catch up quickly.

Dozens of ancient hobnail boots hang from rafters and grainy black-and-white photographs of Hillary and Tensing stare out at a less heroic age. The hewn slate floor and the panelled walls have changed little since scaling Everest was planned on the bar tables. In cases behind glass there are wooden-handled ice-axes, climbing ropes from another century, an early oxygen tank, brown rucksacks and tin mugs. Legends leap from the shadows. A sepia photograph from 1894 of a whiskered and waistcoated fellow tells the story of man's long struggle with the mountains. Another display features maps, woollen hats, a string vest worn by Lord Hunt, a straw hat worn by George Bund, the silk gloves of Sir Charles Evans, the goggles, penknife and umbrella from George Lowe. Expeditions in those times were carried out in a certain style. A shrunken

Steve Lewis

human head from Peru belongs to another world that still had more mysteries than certainties.

Jane Pullee, the owner, grew up here; her parents were hosts to Hunt, Hillary and Tensing. Tonight it's Jamie Owen and a television crew – standards are slipping. We escape the public bars of exhausted climbers slouched on old leather sofas and enter the doorway marked 'Private', a walk back in time. Thankfully this place has been protected from the improvements that would have been inflicted by a large hotel chain. There's a splendid Victorian bathroom complete with a turn-of-the-century jacuzzi spraying from the sides of the shower. (I'm quite sure that would defrost you after an unkind day on Snowdon.) The toilet looks as if it was built by Rolls Royce, and in the wall there's a bell pull to summon the servants, though for what task, I'm not clear, and decide not to ask.

Jane's a mine of living history and remembers some legendary characters. On hearing of the successful

Left: Jane Pullee;
Above: Pen-y-Gwryd

PEN-Y-GWRYD: TRAINING FOR EVEREST

Pen y Gwryd today, and the successful Everest team in 1953.

Everest was not always the goal of those who trained here. The most amusing – and self-disparaging – account of coming to Pen-y-Gwryd to train is by Eric Newby in *A Short Walk in the Hindu Kush*. Newby and Hugh Carless decided to climb in Nuristan but with virtually no suitable experience they needed to learn some basic skills – fast. They arrived at Pen-y-Gwryd in the early morning having driven overnight from London:

'The first thing that confronted us when we entered the hotel was a door on the left. On it was written EVEREST ROOM. Inside it was a facsimile of an alpine hut, done out in pinewood with massive benches round the walls. On every side was evidence of the great ones of the mountain world. Their belongings in the shapes of ropes, rucksacks, favourite jackets and boots were everywhere, ready for the off. It was not a

museum. It was more like the Royal Enclosure. Sir John and Sir Edmund might appear at any moment.' Newby and Carless spent the next few days on some of the classic climbs in the vicinity instructed by a middle-aged doctor and three of the waitresses at the hotel – who had taken the jobs to pursue their love of climbing. After less than a week they set off for the 20,000 foot challenges of the Hindu Kush.

conquest of Everest, which had been planned and exercised here, Chris Biggs, a respected mountaineer who was staying at Pen-y-Gwryd that night, ran through the hotel in the early hours, banging on all the doors to wake the residents for a toast to Hillary and Tensing.

'Anyone who wasn't down in five minutes was threatened with having to leave without breakfast. After a heavy celebration a party of climbers left here at 1.30 am to climb Snowdon.'

Back in the bar, the ceiling boasts a collection of signatures of mountaineers who've stayed here over the years, including Hillary, Tensing and Noel Odell, a member of Mallory's 1924 expedition to Everest. On another continent, decades before tonight, Odell caught a glimpse of Mallory and Irvine through a momentary clearing in the clouds on the day they disappeared, making him the last person to see them alive. Strange to think they all sat around the table here and drank into the early hours.

They were a hard bunch of men who once propped up this bar: they chose to risk their lives in the name of adventure and discovery. And there's still one of the old gang around. He's John Jackson, 84 years of age and he's in the other bar. I'm about to spend several captivating hours in the company of one of mountaineering's last great heroes. John was a reserve climber in Hillary's successful climb of Everest in 1953.

I ask him what motivates people to risk their lives to climb a mountain.

'Because it's there. I'm terrified at the prospect of getting into a racing car and couldn't do that. But in

Talking to mountaineer John Jackson

mountaineering, when you are walking on the roof of the world and you look down upon beauty, and up at a blue sky, it's the most spiritual feeling. There's a feeling that you're among the gods, and all is well with the world'

I suppose all danger is relative. John was part of the first successful ascent of Kanchenjunga in Nepal, the third highest mountain in the world. He is passionate about the outdoors, having spent his life training young climbers in the hills around Snowdonia. But his biggest struggle is yet to come: John is fighting leukaemia, thought to have been brought on by a lifetime's exposure to the sun at high altitude. Just occasionally in life you know that you are in the presence of greatness, and this meeting has been one of those occasions for me.

Sunday morning in Snowdonia brings the scorching day that was forecast. I'm not much good at early mornings but rising today at dawn and looking through the window at blue skies is the most uplifting feeling. There are no yawning complaints from the crew as we

There we stood on the Wyddfa, in a cold bracing atmosphere, though the day was almost stiflingly hot in the regions from which we had ascended. There we stood enjoying a scene inexpressibly grand, comprehending a considerable part of the main land of Wales, the whole of Anglesey, a faint glimpse of part of Cumberland; the Irish Channel, and what might either be a misty creation or the shadowy outline of the hills of Ireland. Peaks and pinnacles and huge moels stood up here and there, about us and below us, partly in glorious light, partly in deep shade. Manifold were the objects which we saw from the brow of Snowdon, but of all the objects which we saw, those which filled us with most delight and admiration, were numerous lakes and lagoons, which, like sheets of ice or polished silver, lay reflecting the rays of the sun in the deep valleys at his feet.

George Borrow (1803-1881) *Wild Wales*

Crib y Ddysgl and Crib Goch

Jeremy Moore

Llyn Padarn and Pass of Llanberis

load up the Landrover. Our climb will offer splendid views for miles in every direction, and there couldn't be a better day for this adventure.

We head for Llanberis. The twin lakes of Llyn Padarn and Llyn Peris cut through the mountain range creating the ruggedly beautiful Pass of Llanberis. From the village, you can catch the little train up the highest mountain in England and Wales or choose one of the many routes to walk to Snowdon's three-thousand-foot summit.

Llanberis is also home to Pete's Eats, a kind of human service station, a temple for outdoor types. None of us is under any illusion how exhausting the day will be, so finding an enormous cooked breakfast for everyone is the first priority. Pete's café is just the kind of place that Snowdonia spawns: it'll never make any money but there's a map-lending library, a book-swapping shelf, free juke-box, pint mugs of tea, and prices so low that it borders on charity. There are a few bleary-eyed walkers in already, ordering full Welsh breakfasts and industrial strength tea – and in the far corner, a familiar face: writer and broadcaster Stuart Maconie.

Now why one of the country's most respected rock music journalists would be sitting in a café in north Wales at this hour is something I'm keen to discover. He's a legend in radio and television broadcasting, though he cut his teeth on NME and Q magazines. His memoir of his life in the music business, *Cider with Roadies*, is on the second-hand bookshelf within reaching distance of our table, but I might embarrass him if I ask him to sign it.

I never know what to expect when you meet famous people: some are distant and difficult (they're usually the ones whose careers are on the skids) but the real stars are usually friendly, affable company, which makes you feel as though you've known them all your life. Maconie is one of the latter. Over heaving plates of breakfast which would give a doctor a coronary, Stuart reveals himself to be a closet mountaineer. It's an odd pastime for a man who's spent his career loitering in dark, smoky caverns reviewing rock groups but he says, the physical challenge and struggle of the hills is just the tonic after a week spent locked in studios. He's never climbed Snowdon and has chosen a different route from us today, but we agree to walk part of the way together. He is wonderful company and soon a delicious stream of indiscretions and anecdotes flow. Breakfast over, we don rucksacks for the walk to the foot of the mountain.

The morning is already warm and it's not yet nine o'clock. We walk past the 'Electric Mountain', one of the modern industrial wonders of Wales. This massive

Above: Pete's Eats; below: with Stuart Maconie at Llyn Padarn

Clogwyn station, Snowdon Mountain Railway

hydroelectric power station is built inside the mountain, in what is said to be the largest underground chamber ever excavated by man. On a wet day in Wales it would be the perfect distraction but, in today's sunshine, it would be a sin to be anywhere other than out on the mountainside.

As we round the corner before Llanberis railway station, an ear-splitting sound makes us all jump and nearly drop the camera equipment. It's the screeching whistle of the steam engine, waiting for the first passengers of the day on the Snowdon Mountain Railway, and then the most pungent stink follows. It's the smell of the smoke which rises in an acrid yellow and purple pall. I don't remember the age of steam trains, but as small boys my brothers and I were fascinated with them and had an attic full of model railways. We're planning to catch the train down Snowdon this evening, our reward for conquering the summit.

The railway line was unveiled in 1896, the only public rack-and-pinion railway in Britain. It had been designed as a tourist attraction, but its début run was marred by disaster when an engine ran away and derailed. In a panic, one of the passengers jumped from the still moving train and fell beneath the wheels.

The car parks of Llanberis are already full. Hundreds of people have, like us, watched the weather forecast and headed here to climb a mountain today. We watch the Snowdon Mountain Railway wheeze its way out of the station loaded with passengers, its progress not much quicker than ours on foot at first. Our adventure up Snowdon is about to begin.

They say you can experience all four seasons in as many hours in Snowdonia, and today couldn't be more different from yesterday's miserable gales. Sunshine slowly burns through the morning to create almost perfect blue skies, and the moss-green hills are dappled by the dark shadows of a few disappearing white clouds. Expecting the worst, we've all come equipped with full waterproofs, fleeces, pullovers and woolly mountaineering hats but, this morning, shorts would have been a better choice of attire. My rucksack already weighs heavily.

In early excitement and ignorance of the gradient to come, children and family dogs run in front of us and then back to their parents and then up the hill again. If they keep this up they'll have climbed Snowdon six times in one day. This part of Snowdonia looks like wild country, but during the summer it is seldom silent country; the steam railway punctuates any stillness with its constipated chugging as it passes over Afon Hwch viaduct.

Spread out in front of us for a mile or so, a line of bobbing T-shirts and gaudy backpacks snake up the footpath. The babble of our earlier excitable conversation has slowed, and each of us has quietened as the climb gets longer. After an hour, it's time for a breather, a swig of water and a sit down.

Dafydd Morris is leaning over his farm gate which borders the footpath from Llanberis. He's farmed these hills all his life. He was out milking at dawn so the day is half over for him. The Right to Roam legislation comes into force today, and Dafydd is dismayed. Whilst he loves people coming to enjoy Snowdonia, in practice he says the change in the law means that anyone can

Bank Holiday walkers

now walk across his private land and worry his animals. He tells us to sit for five minutes and count how many dogs off their leads pass us and then run after his lambs. Sure enough, before five minutes are up, we've counted up to seven dogs off the lead, and half of them run after the livestock in the fields on either side of us. He's clearly dismayed and bewildered as to why some members of the public are so thoughtless.

As we get up to go, I look back down the mountain at the long ribbon of visitors heading up here. This may be the great outdoors, but on Bank Holiday weekend, there are a great many people here too. Our country's wildernesses are where we flock to when we want to escape each other – only to find that everyone else is there too.

Stuart parts company with us. Not for him the main tourist route; he's heading for a shorter, steeper path, quieter but even more challenging, one for the climbing connoisseur. He's been great company and we watch him disappear until he's a tiny fleck of electric blue fabric on the horizon.

SLATE QUARRIES

For most of the people of Snowdonia, these mountains have not been playgrounds, but resources from which a livelihood had to be wrung. The vast slate quarries and spoil heaps which line the north shore of Llyn Peris are a reminder that Snowdonia was once one of the industrial centres of Wales from where millions of tons of slate were exported all over the globe. Slate from here was shipped in great sailing vessels from Port Penrhyn, Caernarfon and Port Dinorwic (Y Felinheli). Padarn Lake Railway, now a great favourite with tourists, is the remains of the all-important rail link between Dinorwig quarries and the port.

Work in the quarries was hard and dangerous – the museum and miners' hospital at Llanberis illustrate this very realistically. Labour relations were sometimes acrimonious and at the Penrhyn quarry a dispute in 1900 led to a lock-out which lasted three years and viciously split a community as loyalties

were tested. Inevitably some men found the hardship their families faced unbearable and returned to work – only to be despised as blacklegs.

What was perhaps most remarkable about the slate industry was the popular culture and desire for self-education which existed among the quarrymen. Jim Perrin has written and broadcast extensively about Wales and Snowdonia in particular; in an essay on the Caban – the quarrymen's hut or shelter – he described the activities and the subjects discussed in one such workmen's refuge in 1902. The men enjoyed singing, recitations, word games, talks on religion, education and their personal experiences; and this was all the more remarkable because it 'took place in dank tunnels, in crude huts two thousand feet up a mountain, in rain and wind, as the men slaked their thirst with bottles of cold tea and ate probably no more than dry bread'.

Three more hours climbing ahead, and I'm enjoying this. I know that tomorrow I'll hardly be able to move I'll be so stiff from walking all day uphill but it's satisfying. I can feel a burning sensation across my shoulder where my rucksack is weighing, and a dull heat up the back and front of my thighs. It is not without a little relief that, after two hours, we sight the Halfway Café. The prospect of a sit down for half an hour couldn't have been sweeter. There is a certain embarrassment in being overtaken by a party of schoolchildren on a walk like this, but nearly all the walkers heading to the summit – at all speeds – have paused a while to refuel here.

The Halfway Café looks like the United Nations. In one corner six Kenyan students are swigging diet Coke, a family of Indians politely share a plate of ham sandwiches, and two girls, clad from head to toe in black burkas, shelter from the midday sun. So many nations of the world united – on the side of a mountain in Wales one summer's day, in the common pursuit of a pot of tea, Welsh cakes and a pee. How marvellous.

Alwena Jones is making sandwiches as fast as the punters eat them. She's farmer Dafydd's daughter. (Well, this is Wales – what did you expect?) She has no electricity or generator up here, and all the food and drink supplies have to be packed onto a quad-bike and driven up the mountain. Alwena herself walks up here to work every day. It must be the maddest catering enterprise on Earth, but I've never savoured every morsel of sandwich and cake so much. The Ritz couldn't have offered better.

We sit down outside the café a moment more to sweat, swig water and watch the world go by. And all the

Alwena Jones at her Halfway Café

world does go by here. An estimated six or seven million people visit Snowdonia every year and it feels as though most of them are walking past me. You might say that Snowdonia's riches have always been exploited: in the nineteenth century copper, lead, zinc and slate workers took their materials from the mountains. Today the commodity is scenery in the sun.

This really is landscape to leave you open-mouthed. Having never been up here before I am dumbstruck by its beauty, scale and majesty. Even so, as I watch the little trains ply their trade up and down the slopes laden with passengers too timid to venture on foot, at this moment I'd happily jump on-board and join them. We're only halfway up Snowdon and I'm pole-axed.

Rucksacks on and I can feel myself starting to lean forward now to compensate for the sudden steepness of the track. A little further up, just before Clogwyn, I meet with Nikki Wallis. Nikki is the Snowdonia National Park's only woman ranger. She looks as you'd expect, a wonderful advertisement for outdoor life,

Above: Snowdon summit;
below: Nikki Wallis

Steve Lewis

blonde and healthy-looking with clear skin. (We've been spotting the walkers who work all week in offices on our way up.) She talks me through the names of the mountains we can see opening in front of us. She enthuses about Clogwyn Du'r Arddu as though its black volcanic face was an old friend. Nikki has climbed all over the world, most recently in Pakistan, but this place is home. When she was little, she says, her parents treated these mountains like their back garden. She's a member of the mountain rescue service and the search and rescue dog team. I can see why they're so successful when it comes to finding lost walkers: these people know Snowdonia like you or I know our own streets. Nikki's radio bursts into life with a garbled reminder that playground this may be for us today, but someone somewhere is lost in Snowdonia, and one family's day out has now become a heart-wrenching ordeal. There's a rescue beginning a long way from here and we part company while Nikki goes off to join the search effort. Even on a perfect summer's day like this, given the number of visitors, I guess it's inevitable that there will be accidents on Snowdon. Heart attacks, dehydration, broken ankles and walkers getting lost are all to be expected before nightfall. The crew members make a mental note to be rescued by Nikki if the worst befalls us.

We still have at least an hour and a half's walking to get to the summit. We've been stopping regularly to film the cloudless scenery and to interview climbers for our television programme. A quick look back down the path reveals that we are the last of the ragged line of walkers heading for the top. All day we've been passed or we've been passing others, and now the numbers have thinned

Glaslyn and Llyn Llydaw below the summit of Snowdon

to almost nothing. A quick calculation throws up the possibility that, at this pace, we may narrowly miss the last train from Snowdon's summit and face a walk all the way back down to Llanberis. It's a lot to ask a television crew to walk up a mountain laden with equipment, and they've done it with extraordinary grace on a boiling hot day, but the understanding was that we would catch the last train down. We quicken our pace – but because we all know that, even if we each live to be a hundred, the chance of capturing a beautiful day like this on film again is so unlikely, we keep stopping and filming some more.

Tantalisingly close, the summit comes into view for the first time, and like in all the movies, the whistle sounds for the last train. It's decision time: catch the train or walk for another half an hour and film Snowdon's peak. The latter option means a four- or five-hour walk back to Llanberis. But there's no discussion or argument. Everyone stays on the mountain and a collective smile breaks out among us. We'll climb Snowdon whatever it takes. The driver, fireman and conductor lean out of the red and cream train and motion frantically for us to run – they are expecting us and they've held our tickets. But our minds are made up and they leave in disbelief that anyone would voluntarily carry filming kit back down the mountain having already carried it up. All the passengers in the carriage turn and wave.

There is no longer any point in walking fast: we have all the time in the world, and I feel a sense of quiet relief that the end of this day won't be timetabled after all. For the first time since we left Llanberis, there are no more crowds, no more long lines of walkers straggling down the mountain. There are only a dozen or so people left within a mile radius of us, all of them hardened mountaineers who clearly intended to be up here after the last train.

With every step I take to the summit, I can see more: Bardsey Island at the tip of the Llŷn peninsula, then the port of Holyhead and the departing ferry to Ireland. They are all miles away, but at this height, I feel as though I could reach out and touch them, as if I had unfurled a map. Just yards from the summit, I stop and stare out from the mountain's ledge and look over to Tremadog Bay and the Irish Sea, bluer than I've ever seen it, flashing the sun's evensong back to the sky. This is the heaven of Wales, the roof of the country. As a little boy on holiday here, I was told that this is where the giants live. And I believe it. This is another Wales, a different country from the one where I grew up. The scenery is bigger, the skies are larger and the scale is grander. Snowdon dominates the landscape for miles around. The surrounding countryside is far below, flat on its face, kneeling in homage to the majesty of the mountain.

The conquest of Snowdon

The last steps to the summit of Snowdon are beautifully hewn. I don't know what I'd expected to grace the top, but I think I'd envisaged a symbolic pile of stones, but of course, this peak is conquered so many times a day, it has to accommodate dozens of visitors at once. By the time I have conquered it, and pulled myself up the last few inches of Snowdon's 3,560 feet, I can hardly string a sentence together for tiredness. But words are unnecessary when you reach the top. The crowded paths of the day are empty beneath my feet. The chatter of excited day trippers has been replaced by the gentle buffeting of the evening breeze off the Irish Sea; the green slopes of daylight are turning golden in the first moments of a sunset the like of which I will wait years to see again.

Fifty-two years ago today, Edmund Hillary and Tensing Norkay set off from camp and climbed steadily after a bitter and desolate night. Hillary wrote:

'I continued hacking steps along the ridge and then a few more to the right . . . To my great delight I realized we were on top of Mount Everest and that the whole world was spread out below us.' Tensing and Hillary had reached the highest point on Earth. That was May 29th, 1953.

I feel a wave of humility thinking of those men who trained here on Snowdon, testing the oxygen tanks that would advance the cause of mountaineering around the world. And I think of how John Jackson, one of the Everest team, would smile at my small triumph.

I've done it! I can finally say I've climbed Snowdon, all three and a half thousand feet of it. I will no longer be the Welshman who hasn't climbed the big one. I didn't go on the train, I walked up, every foot of the way. And, do you know, I feel a sense of childlike excitement and pride. I know it's not Everest but it is the highest mountain in England and Wales and I've climbed it. What's more, now that we're faced with spending the night unexpectedly walking back down the mountain, this has turned out to be twice the adventure I was expecting. I'm so glad I missed that last train.

This is one of the most beautiful evenings any of us can remember, and none of us can bear to get up to leave just yet. There's a reverential silence brought on only partly by exhaustion. They say Rhita, the giant ogre vanquished by King Arthur, lies buried beneath these stones and that Arthur's knights still sleep in these mountains. Tonight, I can well believe in fairy tales and ancient myths. If those heroes of legend will be found anywhere in the world then it will be here.

Steve Lewis

Llanberis Pass at sunset

ON THE WRITER'S
TRAIL

NIGHTFALL

Silence brought by the dark night: Eryri's
Mountains veiled by mist:
The sun in the bed of brine,
The moon silvering the water

CYFNOS

Y nos dywell yn distewi, – caddug
Yn cuddio Eryri,
Yr haul yng ngwely'r heli,
A'r lloer yn ariannu'r lli.

Gwallter Mechain (1761–1849)
trans. Tony Conran

Jeremy Moore

Llyn Peris and Llyn Padarn

ANGLESEY

Steve Lewis

A PASSAGE TO IRELAND

I've sailed around the island of Anglesey several times and from the sea it looks mesmerising, its wild beaches a sight to behold. I shall be crossing the sea to Ireland this time – and on a ferry rather than a sailing boat – but before I make for the port of Holyhead there's a round-about route I want to explore.

Menai Bridge

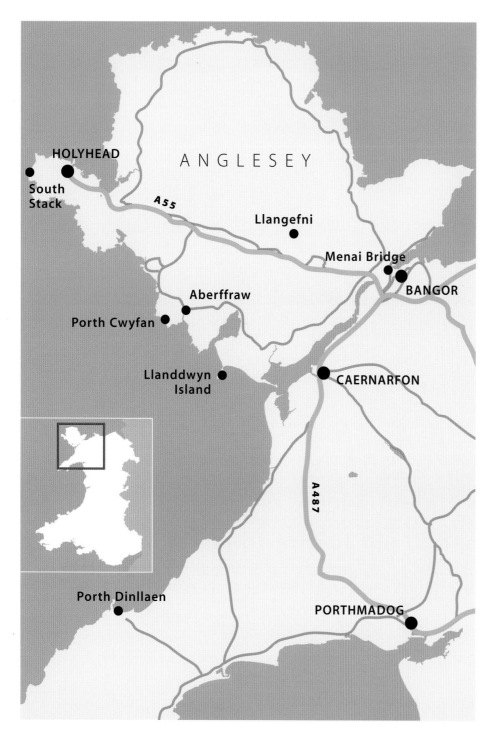

I BEGIN THIS JOURNEY ON THE MAINLAND, at a renowned beauty spot. I'm sitting in the Landrover on the beach at Porth Dinllaen listening to the early morning shipping forecast on the radio. It's the dark before dawn. Because my plan is to take the ferry to Ireland, this is one of those few moments in broadcasting where the words from the wireless will dictate my actions, at least for the next few days. Heavy weather in the Irish Sea would mean that we would have to delay our filming trip.

'Now the shipping forecast issued by the Meteorological Office at 05-05 on Saturday. There are warning of gales in Hebrides, Dogger and German Bight.'

I can reel off the words as though I were still in the bunker at Broadcasting House. Fifteen years ago it would have been me sitting there as a trainee newsreader and announcer on Radio 4 on the red-eye shift, learning the ropes. When you were the new boy or girl you were eased into the world of live broadcasting with delightful overnight shifts that began at 1800 hours the night before. The stint included the late-night shipping forecast and the national anthem long after midnight, and then after a few hours of bleary sleep – which was always fitful because of the quantity of black coffee needed to sound awake beforehand – the alarm would sound at 0430 hours to rouse you for the early shipping forecast before the *Today* programme. Peter Donaldson, the doyen of Radio 4, was my mentor and in his role as chief announcer he often helped me wile away the precious minutes intended for shut-eye in the bar of the Langham, putting the world to right over too many glasses of wine.

The shipping forecast would be telexed over to the BBC from the Meteorological Office in Bracknell. The audience listening all over Europe never knew that the longest broadcast in the world – ten minutes in duration – was read from old cardboard shirt-packing, with the flimsy telexes pinned tightly to the card so as to stop the rustle of loose paper being picked up by the microphone. If listeners had known those practical details, then perhaps some of the magic and poetry of those distant sea-thrashed place-names would have been lost. When I first started broadcasting I wondered who, apart from me, would be mad enough to get up at this time of the morning to listen to the radio. But over the years sackfuls of mail from night-workers, lorry drivers, shift-workers, prisoners and just lonely people, all testified to the millions of people who need the radio for company as much as for the information it imparts.

This morning, I'm waiting for the shipping forecast for the Welsh coast regions.

'Irish Sea and Lundy' – at last, and there's a clear window of good settled weather for our dash to Ireland on the super ferry from Holyhead to Dún Laoghaire.

If history had been different I wouldn't have to drive across Angelsey to Holyhead at all. The sea traffic to Ireland from Wales might have been routed through this beautiful little village instead. In the 1830s Porth Dinllaen was one of the contenders to be the main mail port from north Wales to Dublin. The entrepreneur and MP William Maddocks was Porth Dinllaen's champion; he wanted Westminster to confer the big time on this seaside village on the Llŷn peninsula. It was already a busy little harbour with a healthy number of

Steve Lewis

Porth Dinllaen at dawn

cargo vessels using its sheltered shores. But its chances of becoming the preferred route from London to Dublin took a hammer blow when Holyhead won the day on account of its rail connection.

Not so much a tale of two cities but a story of the fate of two communities. Holyhead prospered and became the busy ferry port it is today, and Porth Dinllaen just carried on quietly doing what it had always done, left behind in the quirks and slipstream of history. In early light, in brisk winds, the spray-lashed empty cottages look as though they've been cast for a role in some romantic drama. The stone arches are home to upturned dinghies, brought out of the water to save them from heavy sinking waves, and the doorsteps of the houses are covered in sand. I feel as though I've walked back to another century.

These days the National Trust is guardian of the village, which has been beautifully preserved. But in its heyday six hundred vessels dropped anchor here. There

Steve Lewis

Lifeboat station

The lifeboat started here in the nineteenth century. In a severe gale in 1863, 18 ships sheltering in Porth Dinllaen were driven ashore and wrecked. Robert Rees of Morfa Nefyn tied a rope around his waist and with the help of four other men rescued a total of 28 lives. A few days later the Rev. Owen Lloyd Williams of Boduan wrote to the RNLI in London and outlined the case for a lifeboat on this busy and dangerous stretch of coast.

Members of the lifeboat crew are just changing into waterproofs, life-jackets and boots. It's only an exercise today but as the beautifully polished vessel drops down the slipway into the angry-looking water, I can't help feeling an enormous sense of humility at the courage of those who at any moment could be called out to help a mariner in distress. It takes a certain sort to want to put the gear on and go to sea when everyone else is heading for land.

Once the equipment has been checked, the exercise done, the lifeboat is hauled back up the slip and for the crew it's time for a lunchtime beer. The crew at Porth Dinllaen are the only completely Welsh-speaking crew in Wales, though even I can catch the gist of their destination this time.

A spiral of smoke winds from the chimney of the Tŷ Coch Inn and the smell of soup and hot pies greets us at the door. Leaning in the corner, the grandfather clock made by R. Thomas of Caernarfon says its ten past ten, as it has been here for the past thirty-seven years. There's a fire burning and we all gravitate towards it to thaw out. Hanging from the rafters are navigational lamps, fishing rods and oar rowlocks, safe now from a life at sea. A handful of walkers who've braved the miles

was a flourishing ship-building business on the coast serving the slate trade, and the fishing trade thrived as well – the catch was so big in Porth Dinllaen that the fish featured on nearby Nefyn's coat of arms. It was an era when sea transport was king and the infant railway network had yet to strangle the coastal traffic.

The men of the lifeboat are on an exercise today. The lifeboat house is beyond the golf course where tweed-skirted women and partners in Rupert Bear-trousers are defying the worst the Irish Sea can throw at them, already playing an early round on what must be one of the country's most exposed courses. Hitting anything in a straight line this morning will be sheer luck. The lifeboat station windows are covered in grilles and mesh as protection from the worst golfers – imagine surviving another successful rescue mission at sea only to be finished off by a duff shot from the green above the slipway.

of stormed beach steam quietly and, hidden from sight underneath one of the tables, a dog with the most unhealthy cough clears its throat – much to the chagrin of some of the visitors who look for the smoker with such bad manners, but to no avail.

The landlady, Brione Webley, has lived in Porth Dinllaen for 37 years and when she and her husband first came here there was no electricity or water. The walls of Tŷ Coch are built from the ballast of ships, she explains. Today she has no time to tell us the myriad tales of smugglers linked to this spot – the bar is swiftly filling up.

Our road journey takes us next from the loser of the battle to be the thoroughfare to Dublin, to the winner: Holyhead. So we drive across the north of the Llŷn peninsula, pass Caernarfon and cross the Menai Strait to Anglesey, choosing this time to take the older of the two bridges. It was the White Knight who said to Alice,

> I heard him then, for I had just
> Completed my design
> To keep the Menai bridge from rust
> By boiling it in wine.

So wrote Lewis Carroll in *Through the Looking Glass* (1871). This is surely not how Thomas Telford's fine suspension bridge is kept looking immaculate, but whatever they use these days, it works. There couldn't be a more imposing gateway to an island.

I'm going to head first for the beach at Porth Cwyfan, near Aberffraw Bay. As we drive over the brow of the hill past Llangwyfan Isaf, the chatter in the

Above: Tŷ Coch Inn, Porth Dinllaen, below: Menai Bridge

SHIPS AND SHIPPING

One hundred years ago, ports which nowadays see only dinghy sailors and motorboats would have been hubs of industry, for so much cargo went by sea. Coal, timber, slate and lime were carried to and from ports all around the Welsh coast, and Anglesey was on the main shipping route to Liverpool. During the nineteenth century Holyhead also became the main port for services to Ireland. Small wonder, then, that Anglesey witnessed numerous shipwrecks. A snapshot of the shipping around Holyhead in 1900 is provided by the reports in *Y Cloriannydd* – a local newspaper established in 1892– which portrays a busy, expanding port and an alarming number of accidents at sea. In April it was reported that the London and North Western Railway Company planned to improve the facilities for 'the ships from Dublin and Scotland to berth'; in November the company announced

Aled Hughes

it would build 'a new stone landing stage' and the newspaper concluded that 'the outlook for Holyhead is promising'. But the weather had other ideas. In February the steamship *Silverhow* of Whitehaven and the Spanish *Astirello* sought shelter in the port; in July the Cunarder

Campania was involved in a collision in fog off Holyhead with the *Embleton*, eleven of whose crew were drowned and seven saved. Fog was again responsible for a collision in August between the SS *Royton Grange* of London and the *Rhyl* of Cardiff, but there were no casualties. One of the notorious hazards to shipping, the Platters, claimed the *Argenonia* on her way from Rochester to Connah's Quay loaded with bricks in November; later the same month the SS *Magician*, coming from New Orleans to Liverpool with a cargo of cotton, caught fire. Newspapers thrive on disasters and accidents but *Y Cloriannydd* did report happier maritime stories. In April Queen Victoria breakfasted at Holyhead before boarding the royal yacht on her way to Ireland; in November, a new steamship for the ferry service, the *South Stack*, made her maiden voyage.

glyndavies.com

glyndavies.com

Landrover stops. In the centre of the spectacular bay beneath us lies the sea-bound church of St Cwyfan. The tiny church stands on an island of its own, an island off an island, erosion over the years having cut it off from the beach. The church dates from the seventh century, though the present structure is Victorian. They still hold services here in summer when the congregation don't mind getting their feet wet. But today, as we get out of the Landrover, an icy breeze has all of us reaching for fleeces and gloves.

We're here to film the landscape photographer Glyn Davies, who is opening an exhibition at Menai Bridge. His exhibited work is all shot within a ten-mile radius of Holyhead. He shows up bright and cheery, brimming with enthusiasm for a few hours' filming on the beach. The crew eye his headgear first with amusement and later with deep jealousy as the day gets colder and colder.

It would be difficult to find a more perfect setting for filming a discussion about landscape photography. The sun moves around the back of the chapel on the island, lighting the beach with flashes of gold. Glyn clicks and whirrs away and every so often stops to show me his pictures on his digital camera. He is as interested in capturing the sculptures the streams leave in the sand as he is in the bigger picture of chapel, beach and cliffs. He turns his attention to the side of the chapel where the graves once fell into the encroaching water and begins another volley of snapping and shaping the landscape.

We leave Glyn to his cameos and retreat to a warm place where we can plan tomorrow's ferry journey to

Ireland and get a good night's sleep – before another uncivilised start to catch the dawn light. Who said it was a glamorous life in television?

At six o'clock in the morning any idea of filming a sleepy Holyhead harbour before first light turns out to have been misplaced: like all busy ports this place never sleeps. We drive through the car park and a security man in a big hat barks at us to stop filming in the port. 'It's against the rules,' he says. Beside us, on the white-laned tarmac, are a line of bleary-eyed truckers, coaches full of passengers still asleep, and cars full to bursting with luggage and excited children. It's hardly a top security scene.

Traders and travellers have been crossing this stretch of the Irish Sea for hundreds of years. Once this voyage would have taken more than a day, even if the wind was blowing in the right direction. By steamship and, later, conventional ferries, the journey time was cut to a few hours, but today we will power past the breakwater and land in Ireland in an hour and a half, courtesy of the high-speed ferry, the HSS *Stena Explorer*.

On board laden with camera, tripod, sound bag and tapes we run up the steps to film our departure from

Photographer Glyn Davies; Abermenai Point

Aled Hughes

HSS Stena Explorer at Holyhead

port. Within minutes, the engines roar into life and we look down to the jetty expecting to film lots of deckhands heaving berthing ropes off massive bollards but the *Explorer* needs none: it reverses into what is best described as a satellite-guided magnetic dock. Look! No people required.

Soon Salt Island, the pier, breakwater and Soldiers Point slip into small scale and disappear into the freezing grey of the still-early morning.

On such a short crossing there's only just enough time to squeeze in a cooked breakfast. Undeterred by some green-faced passengers looking longingly at the horizon for sight of dry land, we troop into the café. All around us travellers, truckers and tourists are sound asleep already, open-mouthed and tranquilised lest the Irish Sea has horrors in store for them. They need not have worried: it's flat calm today.

After breakfast there's only half an hour left before we dock, so we head for the bridge to film our arrival in Ireland. We're taken through coded locked doors to deter those who might hijack a ferry. I've been looking forward to this part of the trip very much. I think it's probably a male thing, but the thought of standing in

the bridge of one of the most impressive ships on the seas is too exciting for words. (Female readers, be tolerant now.)

I had expected a Captain Birdseye type, complete with white beard and cap, hanging on for dear life to an outsize ship's helm. But the bridge of the *Explorer* is more akin to the flight-deck of a plane. In a spacious cabin the size of a house, with windows on every side, the master sits, surrounded by computer screens, operating a small joystick that wouldn't look out of place in a computer game. The bridge is full of consoles offering predicted courses, satellite-positioning scans, and close-up camera shots of the bow and stern. The ship's engines are the same as those found in aircraft. The radio snarls into life and the ship's crew talk to the port authorities in Dún Laoghaire.

Very soon the details of our destination come into sharper focus: parked cars on the headland, houses with washing in the gardens, and in the harbour mouth before us, a dozen sailing dinghies playing a game of chicken with the super ferry heading their way.

We're in Ireland, another country. Strange to think that Anglesey is closer to Dún Laoghaire than to

Cardiff, the capital of Wales. In a café on the main street, a tableful of students from Bangor University order huge late breakfasts all round. This is a cheap weekend away for them. Ireland is their second home for a good night out. Outside the window, a priest trying to park in a hurry outside the church opposite, misjudges a bollard on the pavement and rips the wing off his car. Perhaps he was late for confession. I wish I could lip-read; my guess is that his mutterings are not holy.

The Irish are good at making people feel welcome. They are in no hurry to get rid of visitors – they want us to enjoy their country. In short, they want you to spend your time and your money here, and you can't blame them for that. Wales could learn a lot from this natural ability to advertise.

Back on Anglesey, I am more aware than ever of how we might imitate the Irish and persuade visitors to loiter longer and enjoy more of what Wales has to offer. Cars disembark off the ferry and speed away along the A55 as if there were nothing to see on the island of Anglesey at all. If they just stopped awhile, they would be well rewarded.

South Stack is just one of the stunning places worth visiting, and it's only a short drive from Holyhead. I warn you, though, the descent to the lighthouse is not for the fainthearted: 400 stone steps zig-zagging down between vertical cliff faces. And don't forget, you have to climb back as well when your tour of the lighthouse is over. But it's worth it to view this spectacular structure. The lighthouse was built in 1809 to protect mariners from the treacherous rocks on this north-west

Harbour and breakwater from Holyhead Mountain; breakfast; South Stack; Dun Laoghaire harbour

Aled Hughes

Soft air and sunlight enticed us out this afternoon to Porth Cwyfan, a few miles
along the coast. Porth Cwyfan is a bay, a rather tough and untidy bay of rocks,
sand, and shingle, but a place which never fails to produce birds. It is a place of
some curiousness, for jutting up from its waters is a grass-topped islet, fortified all
around by courses of masonry, and on top is a tiny church. On old maps the church
is shown as part of the mainland, but years of wild seas have gradually worn away

the low cliffs of boulder clay, biting deeper and deeper into the land, until now the little church is many yards from the shore, and is joined to the beach by a causeway of shingle and boulders. Today turnstones were hunting the weed by the causeway, burrowing their heads beneath a clump and throwing it over with the utmost vigour. Stones, quite large stones, were treated in the same manner, and there was inter-mittent clatter as the birds hunted. Charles Tunnicliffe (1901-1979), *Shorelands Summer Diary*

glyndavies.com

glyndavies.com

glyndavies.com

Rhoscolyn; Barclodiad y Gawres; sandstone rocks; illustration by Jac Jones

coast of the island. Many of the visitors here today are birdwatchers – and no wonder. An enthusiast points out to me razorbills, fulmars and choughs, and even I recognise the ravens and puffins.

Geologists come here too to marvel at the folded Precambrian rocks. On the huge, dramatic folds on either side of the bridge you can also see beautiful small-scale crenulations superimposed on the larger pattern.

A few miles further down the coast and there's more to intrigue the geologists. The coastline at Rhoscolyn is spectacular, both for its shapes and striking pink-red and white rocks amongst more sombre hues. It's thought that the Precambrian rocks hereabouts were subjected to at least two periods of violent earth movements. The heat and pressure generated by these natural convulsions was so intense that it buckled and fractured the original strata, leaving folds and faults which continue to baffle the experts. All the cliff area between Porthygaran and Traeth Llydan (Silver Bay) has been designated a Site of Special Scientific Interest because of the world class examples of folded rocks to be found here.

You can drop down to the coast from the A55 at almost any point from Holyhead back to the Menai Strait and you will come upon wonders. You don't even have to leave the Landrover, but it's worth taking a stroll to feel the wind in your face and sand between your toes.

They had a giantess on Anglesey – not your common-or-garden giant like they have in other places – and her home is definitely worth seeing. Barclodiad y

Gawres (the Giantess's apronful) is actually a decorated passage grave which sets the imagination racing. Its name comes from the story that the giantess was carrying giant stones in her apron but such was the weight that they spilled out. The five impressive, decorated stones in the chamber bear cup marks, lozenges, zigzags and other symbols the meaning of which remain a mystery. Illustrator Jac Jones, who has his studio in Llangefni, tells me that 'he saw' in the millennium from the top of Barclodiad y Gawres. It was a clear, clear night and he and his wife watched fires burning on hilltops right across Gwynedd. Small wonder that he specialises in haunting pictures of Welsh myths and legends.

For sand in your trainers, I recommend Aberffraw. The dunes reach as high as 30 feet, with sea holly and marram grass seeming to hold the sculptures in place. You can take a path through them all the way down to the beach.

We drive on to Newborough Warren, but only so far. The Forestry Commission has provided a huge car park at the seaward edge of Newborough Forest, and from the backpacks and cool boxes emerging from the cars, I guess people don't just pop back to fetch a hankie. Newborough Warren is a nature reserve – miles of sandy land and dunes overlooking Llanddwyn Bay, ending in Abermenai Point. This is the opening of the Menai Strait and a particularly narrow point.

A walk in the other direction, along the long, golden beach takes us to Llanddwyn Island. Pilot's Cove is a mile of walking-on-sand (to strengthen the calves) from

Terry Beggs

glyndavies.com

Above: ponies on Newborough Warren, below: Abermenai

TWO SAINTS

Aled Hughes

The church in Holyhead is dedicated to St Cybi – the Welsh name for the port is Caergybi – who was born about 490 AD, the son of a Cornish nobleman. In the years following the Roman occupation and withdrawal, Christianity survived only on the western edges of Britain, in Ireland, Wales and Cornwall. Links between these regions and with Brittany allowed the rituals and organisation of this Celtic church to differ quite dramatically from the church in Rome. For two hundred years, missionaries and scholars kept the Celtic faith alive in the west and their achievements and virtues, as recalled in later biographies, often include miraculous powers. Dewi, patron saint of Wales, was among this band of saints.

Cybi travelled first in south-east Wales and then in Ireland before coming to the Llŷn peninsula. He was worldly enough to realize that getting on the right side of the local prince was key to spreading his message and when he met

Maelgwyn of Gwynedd – an unpredictable, violent man – Cybi disarmed him and was granted the site of what became Holyhead for his

Terry Beggs

monastery. Cybi died in 555 and like almost all Welsh saints – 20,000 reputedly – he was buried on Ynys Enlli (Bardsey).

The connection between saints and islands is inescapable – think of Holy Island, Iona, Bardsey – and at the south-western edge of Anglesey lies Llanddwyn, where one of the few women saints is commemorated. St Dwynwen was a contemporary of Cybi and like him was born of a princely father, namely Brychan of Brycheiniog. One of Dwynwen's remarkable feats was to walk across the Irish Sea; not surprisingly sailors in distress prayed to her in times of danger. Other details of her life are scarce but stories of her sanctity were widespread in the medieval period and she became associated with love and lovers; her help was sought by the great poet Dafydd ap Gwilym in his pursuit of Morfudd. Recently there has been a successful campaign to commemorate Dwynwen as the Welsh St Valentine whose feastday is celebrated on January 25th.

the car park but the cottages are delightful. They were built by the Caernarfon Harbour Trust as homes for the pilots who guided vessels in and out of the Menai Strait over Caernarfon Bar. The pilots also looked after the lighthouse before it was automated. Twr Mawr – 'Large Tower' – is situated high on Llanddwyn Island from which you have a marvellous view of the Llŷn peninsula and the three peaks of Yr Eifl. The tower, painted a sparkling white, has been an important landmark since 1824; its light these days is solar-powered.

We're somewhat reluctantly making back for the bridge. Before either of the bridges were built, we would have been deciding which ferry to take to the mainland. The most important ferry at the western end of the strait ran from Y Foel, which is just opposite Caernarfon. Very handy – for going to market or for going to grammar school – until 1953, when it stopped running.

At Moel-y-don there was another ferry terminal, this time going back centuries. It was here that the Romans crossed the strait. A hundred years ago, when the slate industry was flourishing, quarrymen who lived on Anglesey would cross from here every Monday morning to Y Felinheli (Port Dinorwic), from where they would travel by train up to the Dinorwig quarry at Llanberis where they stayed in barracks for a week of hard labour and no home comforts.

Tides and the weather dictated how the ferries ran, but it's much easier for us to plan our leaving – an effortless drive over Britannia Bridge and we're away. But I can't help feeling that our departure from such a beautiful island ought to be just a touch more romantic.

Terry Beggs

Steve Lewis

Above: Y Foel, below: Britannia Bridge

The days of his boyhood were without end. He would play, he would race, he would go to swim in the sea, to row a boat, to fish. Some days in the summer he and his friends would swim in Porth Gof Du, with not a single living soul there to disturb their merriment. How they would sing as they walked over the heath with their swimming costumes under their arms! They knew exactly how to reach the inlet when the tide had filled it with green translucent water.

Llŷn peninsula from Anglesey

And then they would play or climb the rocks to get warm. Sometimes when they were sitting on the rocks eating their sandwiches, a boat or two would sail in from Trearddur and stay awhile before heading for home.

For anyone who lives in Holyhead, the most outstanding views are the mountains of Snowdonia, which stretch from Penmaen-mawr in the east to Bardsey Island in the west, over fifty miles of magnificent mountains.

R.S. Thomas, *Autobiographies*, trans. Jason Walford Davies

DENBIGHSHIRE

Martin Cavaney

LAND OF SONG AND DANCE

Prestatyn is a gateway to the north Wales coastal resorts to which people flocked throughout the 1800s to 'Sea Bathe' – prescribed as an excellent restorative for arthritis and nervous disorders.

From 1848 the Chester to Holyhead Railway delivered tourists in large numbers, but they weren't the first visitors: the Romans came here too. A Roman bath-house excavated in 1984 proves it.

Prestatyn

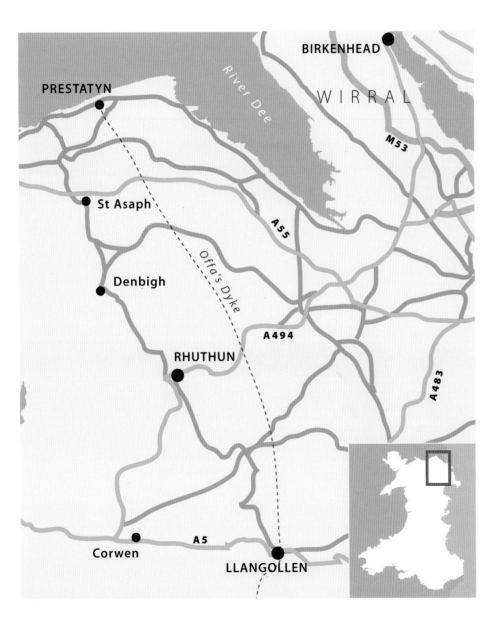

THOSE EARLY TOURISTS WHO CAME TO Prestatyn to enjoy sea air and bathe would do a double take if they stared through their eyeglasses today. Four miles offshore there are 30 turbines spinning away in the North Hoyle Wind Farm. This is Britain's first major offshore wind farm and when fully operational it generates enough electricity to power 50,000 homes. When the project was first mooted, there was considerable opposition but now that it's finished many people acknowledge that the windmills have a certain distant beauty. Rather like bagpipes, perhaps they're best enjoyed at a distance. And they do look much better miles out at sea than plonked in the heart of the countryside.

It would be remiss to visit this part of the Welsh coast without visiting one of the holiday camps that are so much a part of its history. Talk to people in Manchester, Birmingham or the north of England about Wales, and the chances are they or someone they know will have had a holiday here. Millions of tourists have passed through the gates of the holiday camps since they opened more than seventy years ago.

I have to confess that a holiday camp, however popular, wouldn't normally be high on my list of preferred holiday destinations, because I prefer my leisure time to be spontaneous and as far away from large crowds as possible. I don't want you to think I'm a miserable old loner (there's nothing worse than being rumbled this early in a chapter) but, I must confess, I'd prefer root canal dental work without anaesthetic to watching a glamorous granny competition or taking part in a talent contest. I'm not sure that this is what happens in a holiday camp, of course. Apart from watching the fictionalised *Hi De Hi* on television I have absolutely no experience of a camp holiday and have no idea what to expect.

Few would describe Pontin's Prestatyn Sands Holiday Centre as beautiful. Its sprawl of low-rise flats surrounding a central hub owes more to a prison-camp design than that of a hotel. But no one checks in here to listen to talks on architecture. When I say check in, I should tell you that the checkpoint barrier at the entrance and the Stalag 9-like security, makes me think I might be checking out shortly. There's a very high perimeter fence surrounding the whole complex and I'm not quite clear yet whether this is to keep Pontin's residents in, or Prestatyn's mob out. There are no Danger signs, so I assume the fence is not electrified.

Fred Pontin opened his first holiday camp in 1946 and by the 1970s Pontin's was attracting a million tourists to its centres every year. Those early holiday camps were welcome relief for a grey, post-war and still-rationed Britain. The men and women who had been in wartime service no doubt found it easy to adapt to yet more rules and instructions in Civvy Street, even on their holidays. And there were fewer options, in any case. It would be decades before the revolution of cheap airlines and package holidays. In this morning's newspaper there are advertisements offering to fly passengers to the other side of Europe for under £50 and I'm intrigued to know how places like Pontin's survive in the face of such competition. Why would you come here when you could go to Spain, Greece or Turkey for the same money? I've come to find out.

Above: North Hoyle Wind Farm

Wrestling and Bingo at Pontin's

Many guests come here for a weekend or just a few days, the factory-fortnight customers having gone. We don't have that many factories any more. The focus these days is on families, offering around-the-clock care for children, keeping them occupied day and night so Mum and Dad can have a break. To get here, there's no long drive to the airport, no nightmare Greek air traffic controllers' strike and just as long as the kids love it, the parents will too. That's the theory, anyway.

It's a grey day in Wales and someone's forgotten to tell the weather that it's summer. After checking in and finding my chalet, which is in fact a flat, it's time to explore. Everyone's indoors today and the main attraction is wrestling. It's a bit like stepping back into the 1970s. The hall is dominated by a huge ring and the crowds are sitting in their hundreds cheering on the good guy, who's being beaten to a pulp by the baddie. We used to watch the wrestling on the telly with my Dad on Saturday afternoons. He'd have his pipe lit for the occasion and we'd sit entranced while Giant Haystacks and Big Daddy threw themselves at each other, albeit rather slowly, on account of their obesity. Each week my mother would complain that the fights were all fixed. I don't know why wrestling disappeared from the telly: maybe someone like my mother was appointed to a senior job in television and kept saying, 'I'm sure the fights are fixed, you know', or maybe all that violence wasn't politically acceptable. But wrestling is still alive and well in Pontin's.

After an hour or so of splendidly stage-managed wrestling, the hall is cleared for bingo. The announcement is greeted with delighted ripples of applause: you'd have thought we were being offered a safari in Africa. Bingo cards are issued, the caller begins his familiar patter and a hush descends upon the hall. This evening's jackpot is £25. I take my place beside an elderly couple on holiday from Cardiff who loan me a marker pen to highlight the numbers called out. He's a taxi driver and they book into Pontin's centres around Britain because it's a cheap base to explore the surrounding area. This is big walking country: Offa's Dyke footpath begins here and runs 177 miles the length of the Welsh border to Chepstow, but I don't know if many bingo players will be exploring it. At last there's one lucky winner who, by the sound of her squeals, has forgotten it's not the national lottery she's won. She bounces up to receive her cash, delighted and lost for words.

At check-in I've been given a sheaf of information for the coming week. I'm only here for tonight so over the next few days I'll be missing entertainment from ventriloquist Keith Harris and Orville, Timmy Mallet and the Supremes. Later tonight, there's singing on stage provided by the Bluecoats, along with the winners of the talent contest. I thought I'd hate it here, but it's growing on me, slowly.

The film crew have driven four hours before shooting all day and now it's feeding time. The restaurants offer exactly what will keep kids quiet: plenty of fish and chips, burgers and chips or pizzas. Pontin's serve around 1 million meals each year, 35 miles of sausages, 12 articulated lorry loads of chips, 17 tons of cod, and more than a 50-metre swimming pool full of beer. Assistant producer Emma asks for a salad and some fruit and gets a scowl.

Pontin's Prestatyn Sands Holiday Centre

WILLIAM MORGAN'S BIBLE

In the churchyard of St Asaph's cathedral the Translators' Memorial stands as a reminder of the work of William Morgan and others who laboured to bring the Bible to the people of Wales. Born in 1545, William Morgan graduated at Cambridge in 1568 and remained at the university to study Greek and Hebrew. He already knew Latin and, of course, in addition to his native Welsh. Between his ordination in 1568 and 1587 Morgan translated the Bible into Welsh. He had a wide circle of academic friends and enjoyed the patronage of some senior clerics but the translation was virtually all his own work. There had been an earlier Welsh version of the New Testament, the work of William Salesbury who also translated the Book of Common Prayer, but his language was not easy to understand and the Old Testament had not been tackled. After completing his prodigious task William Morgan took his manuscript to

the Queen's Printers in London and in 1588 a thousand copies were published. The government ordered copies of the new Welsh Bible to be placed in every parish church. Morgan was subsequently appointed successively Bishop of Llandaf and of St Asaph, where he died in 1604. It is difficult to exaggerate the significance of Morgan's Bible. Church attendance was compulsory in Elizabethan Wales and congregations soon became familiar with the Word of God expounded in their own tongue. When the great Methodist movement of the eighteenth century took hold, the Bible became an even more important part of worship in chapels. The Welsh Bible also set a standard of literary excellence which had a profound influence on secular writing. Other Celtic countries which, at the time, had no such translation found their languages in decline. In contrast, the survival of Welsh into the nineteenth century and beyond owes more to William Morgan than to anyone or anything else.

Memorial, St Asaph's cathedral

Now for a few beers in front of the cabaret. The concert arena smells of stale beer and fresh cigarette smoke. Bluecoats Russell Quinn and Lucy Jackson join me for a drink; they're both doing the season here and hope, like so many other Blue- and Redcoats before them, that this will lead to their big break into show business. Lucy is a bubbly blonde from Liverpool who just wants to be on stage singing and dancing. Russell, who is from Birmingham, came here as a child on holiday and won the talent contest aged 17. They've spent the day helping children get their faces painted, assisting Captain Crocodile's driving school, encouraging circus skills and supervising jumpers on the trampoline. After a packed day of being surrogate parents to dozens of children, they'll spend their evening singing in the cabaret. They're good company, both driven by a love of entertainment but mindful of how much that world has changed since the great days of variety once dominated television. Great entertainers who can do a song and a dance no longer fill Saturday-night screens.

My bed for the night is on the other side of the complex, among hundreds of others. I was taken on a tour this afternoon of all of the building work on the site. All the flats are being refurbished for the twenty-first century. Microwaves and digital televisions are being fitted in the hope that this will attract another generation of tourists through the doors. The curious thing about the layout is that despite their location, right on the beach of the north Wales coast, many of the chalets face inwards rather than looking out to sea. It's as though what once mattered was the holiday experience, the entertainment within, not the setting.

Pom-poms

Breakfast and it's time for an enormous fry-up. Jon Rees the cameraman suggests he may have to take tomorrow off in preparation for the heart attack he's expecting. We load up and say our goodbyes. I'm in two minds as to what to think of my holiday camp experience. You can knock it and criticise the chips-with-everything fare, the rather run-down fabric and the dated nature of what holiday camps have to offer. Or you can see them for what they are, a cheap and cheerful resort giving the punters what they want. The customer is never wrong and they're queuing to get in. Not every one wants to escape to the sun, plan their own itinerary and choose a different restaurant every night. The majority of clients here are hard-pressed parents desperate to have a few hours when they can take their eyes off the kids. And that's what places like this offer. Whether the holiday camps will survive another generation without a massive reinvestment and reinvention is another matter. But I'm glad I came. I feel as though I've been part of

Dyfed Elis-Gruffydd

Clwydian hills

the north Wales coast story now. I report a twinge in my side and Jon Rees in the passenger seat suggests it's the early signs of that heart attack.

We're spending the morning walking in the Clwydian Hills with Carl Rogers the author of several, guidebooks to this area. At half the height of Snowdon, the hills of Clwyd are shapely and striking, both to the east and west. We climb over the remains of the Iron Age hill-fort at Moel Arthur. It was an extraordinary achievement of civil engineering to excavate such deep trenches and earth walls. Even to this day they are formidable sights and a challenge to scale. From the top, the view over the Vale of Clwyd is spectacular. It's disappointing when the wind and rain announce their imminent arrival, scowling and circling above the lowland fields far off in the distance, between us and Snowdonia. Our filming has to end for a few hours and we head for an early lunch in Denbigh.

Denbigh was once one of the most prosperous market towns in Wales. In Tudor times the place

flourished and was well known for its glove-making and saddlery. It was later the birthplace of Henry Moreton Stanley, the journalist and explorer who was sent to find Dr Livingstone.

Inside Denbigh Castle odd sounds bounce around the ruined walls: there's a scraping, a chipping and the sound of splitting stone. Mial Watkins is supervising his two most experienced masons as they repair a low wall ravaged by hundreds of years of frost and some careless renovators fifty years ago. Well meaning conservationists repaired these walls with concrete, which now has to be replaced with a kinder but more robust mortar, similar to what the original builders would have used. Mial looks and sounds like the actor Anthony Hopkins. He pauses and picks at his words like a *sommelier* choosing fine wines – as befits a man charged with the care and conservation of the historic buildings of Wales. It's an unending task preventing ruins from going to ruin: there's always something that needs doing.

I set off to explore the locked town walls of Denbigh. Trebor Watkins is the castle's curator and, rather like an ancient retainer from medieval times, he emerges from his office with a huge ring of keys. He produces the right key and, as in a scene from a horror film, the iron gate creaks open against the stone of the entrance to the town walls. Thank goodness we're doing this in bright daylight. They started to build the walls in 1282 – constructed before the castle to offer protection to the builders of the keep.

'Rather like the safe zone in modern-day Iraq,' says Trebor. 'You had to protect the workforce.'

Denbigh was the stronghold of Dafydd ap Gruffydd who was awarded the lordship for helping the English defeat his own brother Llywelyn. (Just imagine what their family get-togethers must have been like after that treachery.) Dafydd came to a sticky end and was hanged, drawn and quartered. Denbigh Castle was built on top of Dafydd's original fort, but in its new role the stronghold was built to keep the Welsh under control. There was no more symbolic statement of strong English dominance than building the castle on the site of the old Welsh fort. The construction was interrupted in 1294 when the castle was held for a time by the Welsh. When the builders finally packed up they had left behind an extensive and spectacular structure of both castle and walls. Stretching almost 1 km in length, the walls had been constructed using a technique that involved building two parallel walls and filling the gap between them with stones and hot mortar. This construction technique was to prove significant in 1646 when the castle was besieged by Parliamentarians who realised that their cannon fire was useless against such rock-hard stone walls. Unfortunately, rather than push off home, General Mytton decided to starve the garrison instead. All of which goes to prove you must have the right mix in your mortar – you can tell I've spent too long with the stone masons today.

We walk along the narrow cobbled pathway level with the chimneys and look down into people's gardens. The view is magnificent and Denbighshire's countryside spreads out before us like a tapestry of green. On this sunny afternoon it's difficult to imagine that this was once the sight of siege and destruction. It's odd thinking how someone my age would once have

Denbigh castle, town and walls

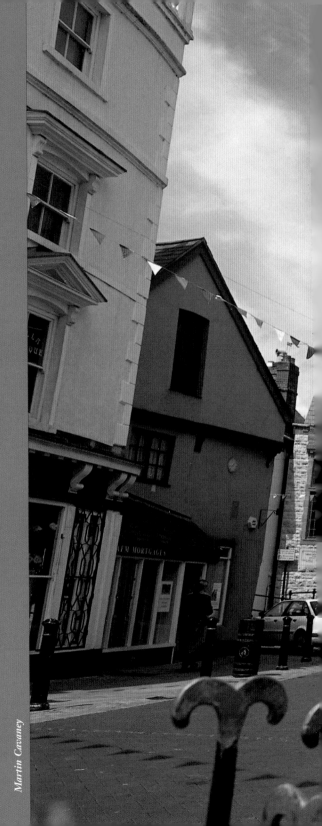

ON THE WRITER'S TRAIL

We visited Denbigh and the remains of its Castle. The town consists of one main street, and some that cross it which I have not seen. The chief street ascends with a quick rise for a great length. The houses are built some with rough stone, some with brick, and a few are of timber. The Castle with its whole enclosure has been a prodigious pile . . . In the chapel (St Hilary's) on Sundays the service is read thrice, the second time only in English, the first and third in Welsh.

from the journal of Samuel Johnson, 1 August, 1774

Martin Cavaney

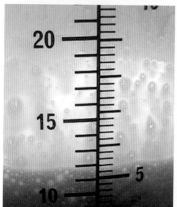

Rhydonnen Farm, milking parlour

stood here and looked out knowing that below were any number of other men, ready to kill him. But that was the nature of this borderland, home to some two centuries of perennial warfare between English kings and Welsh princes. The princes of Gwynedd determined to hold onto their ancient kingdom, and the invading Norman barons trying to contain the Welsh.

The sun's falling over the castle ramparts as we leave. We have a dinner date and it's not in town.

Alan and Buddug Jones and their children live in Rhydonnen, a striking black and white fifteenth-century farmhouse in Llanhychan near Rhuthun, where we'll be staying tonight. It has to be an early night, because tomorrow I have to help out on the farm and their days begin in the dark. Parts of the house date back to 1245. Buddug recently discovered an immaculate wattle and daub doorway hidden for centuries in a wall. She says the 800-year-old yew tree in the front garden leads them to believe the house was once a place of worship. They are custodians of a piece of history that is ancient and beautiful. Like so many farmers in Britain they've had to diversify their business and this farm is no longer all about livestock and crops. The newest branch of their endeavour is to offer farm holidays.

When dawn comes, I don't know who is more nervous, me or the cows. I know that doctors sometimes warm their stethoscopes before placing them on patients' chests – I wonder if a novice milker like me should warm my hands before putting them to the udder. The cows line up, heavily laden and ready to stroll into the milking parlour. I suppose it's an inevitable consequence of being a townie, but I don't really know how to milk a cow – my milk has always come from the milkman. My grandparents had livestock on their smallholding in Saundersfoot and as children we were used to being around cows but never under them.

There's a certain idiocy about agreeing to be filmed by your friends while trying to milk a cow. There is, for example, the possibility that at such close quarters to the animal's nether regions one might be sprayed with not just milk but a number of less palatable substances. Alan is clearly a little worried about having someone as useless as me in the milking parlour, not to mention a tittering television crew, but the opportunity for comedy value was just too much to decline.

Cows have wonderfully expressive faces and just at this moment the expression on the face of the cow closest to me says, 'Help! Whatever you do, don't let that idiot anywhere near my udder.' But there's no going back now for any of us. The first job, as I learn leaning under a cow's backside (rather like the way you check the oil under a car bonnet), is to produce manually a little milk from the teats to check for mastitis – if the teat is blocked the animal needs attention. Oh, it's a glamorous life in television.

Alan is methodical in his master-class but, without trying to race him through the early chapters, I'm keen to stand up straight as soon as possible because Daisy seems not only to have several gallons of full cream inside her, but half a hundredweight of slurry too. Every cow has this manual check by hand before any milking and so far they've all been spectacularly self-controlled.

Daisy

The Horseshoe Pass

So far so good. Reaching the end of the line of cows, I see another dozen lined up ready for checking too. I am in the bovine equivalent of a sharpshooters' alley, with the backsides of dozens of cows lined up level with my head.

The next step is pushing the milking machine suction pipes onto each cow, a process which is semi-mechanised. Four pipes that look like an upturned hand appear near the udder but require manual assistance to be placed over the teats. They only work if placed in the correct order, so the process is a little slower and more delicate than it might sound. Once fitted, the suction from the pipes is sufficient for nature to take its course, and when fully milked, suction stops and the pipes drop off automatically.

Don't ever think cows are dumb animals; they had me sussed out long before we were intimate. My grappling with equipment and distended teats had them trying to kick me out of the way in no time. Still, I manage to escape unscathed – and come to think of it, I'm getting the hang of milking too. Then, as quickly as

it started, all the cows are wandering back to the field a little lighter than when they arrived. The producers would like to point out that no cows were harmed in the making of this movie – well, not much anyway.

It's on to Llangollen next. We're huddled around maps looking for the Horseshoe Pass when someone switches on the radio just before the hour. We break off chattering on hearing the headlines:

'BBC News at 10 o'clock. Four suicide bombers have struck in central London killing 52 people and injuring 700.'

All of us are suddenly wakened from our rural idyll of the last few days and we begin calling friends and family who may have been caught up in the unfolding chaos. Our friend Rob Finighan and his wife Lisa might have used those buses to get to work this morning – but they answer our calls and we gratefully hear that they are unharmed.

Jon Rees says what a lot of people are already thinking: it was bound to happen sooner or later. The rest of the day is spent returning to the cars on the hour to listen to the radio news bulletins. It all seems a long way away from a farm in rural Denbighshire. And yet so close.

As we drive to Llangollen we are for the most part quiet and thoughtful.

'BBC News at 11 o'clock . . . The co-ordinated attacks hit the transport system as the morning rush hour drew to a close.'

There is a certain poignancy to our travels this morning. London is descending into chaos, there are no tube trains or buses and the roads have been sealed off. The capital is looking warily for some suspicious faces – those who would wreak murder on the streets of Britain. The politicians being interviewed on the news are clearly very shaken and it's even more discernible in their voices without the distraction of television pictures. This is a country that is scared and now scarred too. In the name of twisted religion and the politics of hate, innocent men and women have been killed and maimed by men whom they don't know. And in Llangollen at the other end of the country, young people from all over the world have come to sing at a festival born out of the horror of the Second World War.

BBC News at midday. 'Three bombs went off at 08.50 on underground trains just outside Liverpool Street and Edgware Road stations, and on another travelling between King's Cross and Russell Square.'

On the approaches to Llangollen the traffic slows as cars ponder where to park. One wonderful escape from the speed of everyday life would be a slow glide on the canal. A family chugs by in a narrow boat beautifully painted in red and green, its brasswork gleaming. The canal was built to carry slate and goods to the cities of the north of England. Thomas Telford built its famous Pontcysyllte aquaduct in 1795, a work of civil engineering genius that took ten years to complete. The fall of the canal from its source is one inch per mile – imagine the mathematical prowess that delivered that accuracy. I'm told that the mortar used in construction (back to mortar again) comprised of lime, water and oxen blood. To seal the joints, flannel and lead were dipped in boiling sugar.

Above: River Dee, left: Llangollen canal, below: Pontcysyllte aquaduct

THE LADIES OF LLANGOLLEN

In George Borrow's account of his extensive travels, *Wild Wales*, he describes many happy hours spent in Llangollen. He was intrigued by the Ladies of Llangollen and asked the 'old church clerk' to tell him about them. He remembered their first coming . . . their living in lodgings, their purchasing the ground called Pen y maes, and their erecting upon it the mansion to which the name of Plas Newydd was given. He said they were very eccentric, but 'good and kind.' Other comments were not so generous: John Lockhart visited Plas Newydd with Sir Walter Scott and met with two persons wearing 'enormous shoes, and men's hats, with their petticoats so tucked up, that

at first glance . . . we took them for a couple of hazy or crazy old sailors'.

Both ladies hailed from Anglo-Irish landowning families: Lady Eleanor Butler was 41 when she and her companion, Miss Sarah Ponsonby, who was sixteen years younger, moved into Plas Newydd. Having decided to run away and live together, they left Ireland in May 1778 and settled in Llangollen, not only because they loved the countryside around the small town but also on account of the fact that it would be cheaper than living in England. The cottage they rented was renamed Plas Newydd but it was not until 1819 that the two ladies bought the house;

they gradually embellished the exterior with elaborate porches and oriel windows. The mock timber framing was added after their deaths.

Since they were well connected and because Wales was becoming a fashionable destination for wealthy tourists seeking Romantic and Picturesque scenery, the ladies received a stream of notable visitors. Wordsworth composed a poem celebrating the beauty of the situation and the friendship of

Sisters in love, a love allowed to climb
Even on this earth, above the reach of time.
Lady Eleanor died in 1829 aged 90, and Sarah followed two years later.

The traders aboard their narrow boats have long gone, but tourists who navigate the waters love the pace of the waterway.

An ear-piercing whistle makes all of us jump, before the fug from the Llangollen Steam Railway locomotive comes into view. The train is laden with passengers hanging out of their carriage windows, keen to catch every detail. We have no time for a trip on the train today, but just the railway station at Llangollen is worth seeing – it's a real period piece.

Eight hundred feet below Castell Dinas Brân – once one of the most important Welsh fortresses – is the entrance to the International Eisteddfod ground. As we arrive at the entrance to the festival, black, brown, white and yellow faces in their hundreds are gathered in beautiful traditional dress beneath the hills of this dramatic landscape. Last year the festival was nominated by Terry Waite for the Nobel Peace Prize. At the time Waite wrote,

'It is remarkable that the people of a small town in north Wales have been able to sustain the vision of the first Eisteddfod back in 1947 – to help heal the wounds of the Second World War by inviting the world to sing and dance in Llangollen. It is testament to the power that ordinary people can make a difference to the politics of the world.'

Amidst the cacophony of sound not unlike an international railway station, Betty Roberts is trying to help a choir of Kenyans who've lost their luggage somewhere between Africa and north Wales and six Latvians who've lost their passports. The Caribbean drummers, who need somewhere to stay tonight, have

Steve Lewis

Above: Llangollen Steam Railway; below: Station by the river Dee

Llangollen International Musical Eisteddfod

been sorted out and leave beaming. None of it troubles her; she's been working behind the scenes at the International Eisteddfod in Llangollen for forty years.

'In 1980 I had a phone call in the early hours of the morning saying that 67 unexpected Hungarians were waiting to be collected from Ruabon railway station. We knocked doors in Wrexham before dawn, desperately seeking beds for the guests and managed to find them all a bed for the night in two hours flat. The Hungarians were moved to tears.'

Betty's main responsibility is the overseas reception area where Llangollen ladies provide unending supplies of tea and cakes for musicians and dancers who've travelled halfway across the world to be here. Many of the visitors have had the most dreadful journeys across continents, putting up with overland coach journeys lasting days, inevitable trouble at customs with suspicious passport control and often little money. But against all the odds they come here simply to make music with other musicians of the world. In contrast to what is going on at the other end of Britain, here there is kindness shown to strangers, a welcome for foreigners and hospitality offered on trust. There may be no shared language, but there are plenty of grateful smiles for those who offer tea and cake.

We stay and watch singers, dancers and instrumentalists for a few hours. The simple joy of watching with a crowd of a few hundred others performances on an outside stage! It's the young impromptu performers who are the real stars, but during the week the opera singers Lesley Garrett and Willard White will delight ticket-holders in the big tent.

'BBC News at 5 o'clock . . . the final explosion was around an hour later on a double-decker bus in Tavistock Square.'

Making merry at the Eisteddfod

After all the carnage that has taken place today in London, I feel fortunate to have been walking around Llangollen Eisteddfod. On such a day, when your faith in humanity takes a terrible knock, it is some comfort to be in this company. At this festival, itself born out of the end of a terrible war, London's bombing tragedy can be measured against the hope of these young musicians for the future and their practised international harmony. If I had watched the day's events unfold in front of a television screen in the newsroom or at home I would feel even more grimly depressed about mankind and its prospects. But instead, surrounded by the cream of the world's next generation, I feel a tiny measure of optimism. When they inherit this world, it might be home to a generation more at ease with itself and each other. It's time to go home.

ON THE WRITER'S TRAIL

After luncheon we all started for Llangollen, going by rail, and had a beautiful afternoon. The station was very prettily decorated . . . We turned sharp to the left above the station, where there was a Guard of Honour of the Volunteer Battalion of the Welsh Fusiliers, with their band and goat, with its gilt horns (my gift), and drove up the beautiful wooded, mountain-girt, deep valley, dotted with villas and cottages, to Bryntisilio, the well-known residence of Sir Theodore Martin . . . Had tea in the drawing-room, during which a selected number of Llangollen choirs sang Welsh songs, in the pretty sloping garden. It is wonderful how well these choirs sing, being composed merely of shopkeepers and flannel weavers.

from the journal of Queen Victoria, 26 August, 1889

River Dee at Llangollen

Martin Cavaney

ACKNOWLEDGEMENTS

A project like this filmed over so many months in so many places wouldn't be possible without the co-operation of the people who live in the towns and villages we visited and to them my thanks for their patience and good humour. At Aspect Television all the staff who were part of the crew are mentioned in my introduction but back at base, Rob Finighan and Mary Adams were, as ever, the rocks on which a series like this is built. My thanks to Clare Hudson and Martyn Ingram at the BBC for their continuing support for the travel documentaries we've made over the last four years. I must also say a word of appreciation for my editors Gail Morris Jones on *Wales Today* and Julie Barton at Radio Wales who have turned a blind eye to yet another summer of absences from Broadcasting House.

Martin Cavaney's splendid photography has again been a joy. My thanks to a number of other photographers, to Dun Laoghaire Harbour Authority and to Stena Line for kindly providing images and information, to Rebecca Ingleby for her design and to Edward Parry and Dyfed Elis-Gruffydd for being so knowledgeable and generous with their advice. Any errors which remain in the text are my own. Finally Mairwen Prys Jones and the staff at Gomer Press have made the process of quickly writing a book to a tight deadline entertaining and amusing and for that much thanks.

I am indebted to many authors for works of reference which I found fascinating, and recommend the following publications: *An Uprooted Community, A History of Epynt*, Herbert Hughes (Gomer, 1998); *The Menai Strait*, Gwyn Parri Huws & Terry Beggs (Gomer, 2003); *The Ladies of Llangollen*, Elizabeth Mavor (Michael Joseph, 1997); *A Short Walk to the Hindu Kush*, Eric Newbury (Seckter & Warburg, 1958); references to *Y Cloriannydd* are based on *Anglesey 1900*, Margaret Hughes (Gwasg Carreg Gwalch, 2000); Jim Perrin's essay quoted on p.96 is published in *Spirits of Place* (Gomer, 1997).

In order to follow the trails of notable writers, extracts were taken from the following publications: *Letters from Wales*, ed. Joan Abse (Seren, 2000); *Welsh Verse* trans. Tony Conran (Seren, 1986); *Song of the Earth*, Alexander Cordell (new edition Blorenge Books, 1999); *Autobiographies*, R.S.Thomas, trans. Jason Walford Davies (Dent, 1997); *Collected Poems 1958-1978*, John Tripp (Christopher Davies); *Shorelands Summer Diary*, Charles Tunnicliffe (William Collins Sons & Co. Ltd., 1952).